Balance

AT ITS

Best

How to bring order to your hectic life

by Dr. Lori Salierno

Balance at Its Best *by Dr. Lori Salierno is significantly revised and updated from the book that inspired it:* Real Solutions for Ordering Your Private Life *by Lori Salierno (Ann Arbor, Mich.: Servant Publications, 2001 [out of print]).*

ISBN 0-7414-4370-8

All scripture quotations, unless otherwise indicated, are taken from the HOLY BIBLE, NEW INTERNATIONAL VERSION®. NIV®. Copyright © 1973, 1978, 1984 by International Bible Society. Used by permission of Zondervan. All rights reserved.

Scripture quotations marked (NASB) are taken from the NEW AMERICAN STANDARD BIBLE®, Copyright © 1960, 1962, 1963, 1968, 1971, 1972, 1973, 1975, 1977, 1995 by The Lockman Foundation. Used by permission. All rights reserved.

Scripture quotations marked (KJV) are from the King James Version of the Holy Bible.

Cover design: Chris Master & Steve Hammond

Cover photo: Michael Fuller

Edited by: Steve Hammond

Published by:

INFINITY
PUBLISHING.COM

1094 New DeHaven Street, Suite 100
West Conshohocken, PA 19428-2713
Info@buybooksontheweb.com
www.buybooksontheweb.com
Toll-free (877) BUY BOOK
Local Phone (610) 941-9999
Fax (610) 941-9959

Printed in the United States of America
Printed on Recycled Paper
Published March 2008

Contents

Dedication

I want to dedicate this book to the staff of Celebrate Life International. Thank you for the champions of discipline that you are. Your passion for excellence has been a great inspiration. I work with the best people in all the world.

I especially want to thank Dale, Jennifer, Jodi, Joe, José, Joseph, Kathy, Lesha, Robin, Russel, Shawn, Steve, and Wesley.

I love you, CLI Staff—you are my heroes!

Acknowledgments

My heartfelt thanks go to Steve Hammond for his skillful assistance from beginning to end. He is a persistent, patient and competent writer. He researched, edited, and updated all the material that went into this book. I am always impressed by his depth of thought and wise perception. His critiques of my writing added expanded thinking and a fuller approach on the subject of living a life of order.

I also want to thank my accountability group of nine women. They have had a significant influence on my life and have helped me understand the value of a balanced life.

Foreword

On many occasions I have both written and spoken of a particular morning in my young adult life when I reached a point of personal desperation. Suddenly, I went from an enthusiastic, purpose-driven, indefatigable pastor to a mixed-up person who wanted to quit and run from all responsibility. Call it burnout or breakdown, anything you want, but for me it was the day I discovered that my inner life was something I could no longer ignore.

I know the date of that day of desperation because I began writing a journal of my life that very afternoon. It was the first of a stack of journals which I have been writing ever since in my daily quest for a balanced life.

Almost everyone watching my early days of public ministry might have applauded me for my commitment and focus, my willingness to work hard, and my seeming inexhaustible energy. Perhaps the only one close enough to see a deeper and alarming truth was Gail, my wife, who began to realize that if I kept up the way I was living, there were going to be adverse consequences for me, my family, and, ultimately, the church I was serving.

A re-read of that first journal—written almost 40 years ago—reminds me of a life that needed almost everything Lori Salierno has written about in this book. From simple and practical things such as adequate sleep and a vitamin pill to loving friendships and greater spiritual discipline: I needed it all.

That's why I'm glad to commend Lori's *Balance at Its Best*. Few are better equipped to say the things she has written. Lori is a woman blessed with a remarkable vision, extraordinary energy, and an ability to galvanize people together to make great things happen.

But it is clear that, with these qualities, has also come a danger that she recognizes. The danger of achieving good things at the expense of best things. I'm thinking of a well-ordered heart in which God can freely establish His presence, a heart that does not flame-out prematurely, and a heart that reflects the character of Jesus Christ.

Lori's message is not new exactly. Perhaps her way of presenting it replete with wonderful stories and applications of Scripture are unique. But great and godly men and women down through the centuries have seen and spoken of the very same themes that make the heart of a person a strong center out of which can come wisdom and words of redemption.

In fact you can go back to Jesus himself and see the basis of Lori's writing in action. J.B. Phillips—the great theological and Bible scholar of the mid-20th century—wrote:

> It is refreshing and salutary, to study the poise and quietness of Christ. His tasks and responsibility might well have driven a man out of his mind. But he was never in a hurry, never impressed by numbers, never a slave of the clock. He was acting, He said, as He observed God to act—never in a hurry.[1]

These words of Phillips, so masterfully written, came to me as I read through *Balance at Its Best*.

Thus, I urge the reader to a slow and thoughtful "read" of Lori's book, so that nothing will be lost or neglected. Read with a pen and mark key words and phrases with care. Then at the end of each reading, take a few minutes to open your mind and heart to what the Spirit of God may have prepared for you as nudges toward change and personal growth.

We need a few more people around who live the well-balanced life. Perhaps the reading of this book will cause you to want to be one of them.

Gordon MacDonald

Canterbury, New Hampshire

Preface

Six years have gone by since I first penned *Real Solutions for Ordering Your Private Life*. I was excited about that book because I knew I had taken lessons I had recently learned and put them on paper—so I could apply them more deeply in my own life as well as share them with others. I wanted others to see the pitfalls my family and I had navigated around (and some of the ones we had fallen into). I've gotten great feedback from people who read that book. One thing many said was that the advice was pretty hard to put into practice all at once. Admittedly, the book was aimed at making radical changes in our lifestyles so we could glorify God all the more. I suggested to those who read the book to take it in small doses.

Now six years later, I've moved deeper in some areas. This new book under the title *Balance at Its Best* helps you and me navigate these stormy waters even more effectively, with greater depth, and I hope, with more grace.

I have added new material on fasting and about having a spiritual director. The subjects of silence and solitude are more important to me now, so I expanded on those subjects. I've been amazed at how we "fill the gaps" of silence in our lives. When you get in your car, do you ever consider *not* putting on the radio? When you think about prayer, do you only think about talking *to* God? What about taking time just to *listen* to him?

In my speaking engagements, I have often presented the talk "Balance is Beautiful" to complement the original book. Balance *is* a beautiful thing. Our lifestyle will give greater glory to the One who created us as we submit all areas of our lives to

His Lordship. But I noticed that people sometimes misunderstood what I meant by balance. What I *don't* mean is that if we're clever enough, we'll be able to keep all the proverbial plates spinning all the time. Besides, even if I could get my life in perfect balance, others around me will probably be out of balance, and mess up my "perfect" life! No, plates will sometimes come crashing all around us. The key to having balance at its best lies in knowing what to do when they crash. I share candidly in this book about my father. One day *all* his plates fell, and the psychologist in charge told me I was next in line because I was most like my dad. What a wake up call!

This book is designed to help us take the steps necessary to avoid hardships that we'd bring on simply because we've forgotten about certain disciplines designed to grow us spiritually—or we knew about them but never put them into practice. Now it's your turn. Go for it! See the pages ahead as the beginning of an awesome journey that will change your heart—forever!

Lori Salierno, D.Min.

August 2007

Chapter 1

The Race Is On

When I was in the ninth grade, I joined the Shumway Junior High track team. I was a "miler." In my first race I competed against runners from three other schools. We approached the starting line and took our positions. The starter lifted his pistol high and called out: "On your mark! Get set!" Then . . .

Pop-pop!

"Shumway runner jumped the gun!" he shouted. "Let's start again!" Again he lifted the starting pistol in the air. "On your mark! Get set!" Then . . .

Pop-pop!

"Shumway runner!"

"Yes, sir?" I said.

"Do you know how many laps you have to go when you run the mile?"

"Yes, sir," I answered. "Four laps."

"That's right, you have four laps to run. So there's no need to jump the gun. Why are you jumping the gun?"

I proudly called out my answer: "Because I want to win, sir!"

"Shumway runner," he said, "how you start the race is not what's important. What's important is how you finish it."

This was true for a junior-high miler, but it's even truer in all of life. How we start the race is nowhere near as important as how we finish it. Anyone can have an enthusiastic beginning, but few can go the distance. *To do that requires running a balanced race.* It is not good enough to pour our all into one area of life and to neglect the others. No, to run the race successfully, we need to be able to weather disappointments, discouragements, and setbacks and still stay on track.

Is Balance Really All That Important?

Compare imbalance in your life to the ride you get in a car with tires that are out of balance. Can you get where you're going? Yes. But on the way the ride will be bumpy and uncomfortable. It will cause you stress and pain. And there is always the chance that the imbalance will cause a major setback in your trip.

Yet, if you get there anyway, why is balance so terribly important? Because people who lack a sense of balance in their lives lose so very much. Some lose their zeal for God. Some lose their families. Some lose their sanity. Almost all lose their joy.

Well, that's not me, you may be saying. I mean, sure, I do spend too much time at work, and I don't get any exercise, but other than that, my life is pretty well balanced.

Pretty well balanced? That means you have work to do. For you see, if any one area gets out of balance, it automatically impacts and handicaps the others. A lack of balance in one area means a lack of balance everywhere.

Back in the 1800s, there were slaves who, though freed by the Emancipation Proclamation, still chose to live in slavery. Why? Because for them freedom was a frightening unknown.

They were not alone in this. Consider the Israelites in biblical times who were freed from their slavery in Egypt. Very soon they were longing for the leeks, garlic, and cucumbers they ate in captivity. They were willing to go back to Egypt and become slaves again just to satisfy their appetites!

This is one of the great dangers of imbalance. Once we get used to it, it seems comfortable enough to us. We put up with the bumpy road or the pain and stress the ride causes, because it's all we know. We assume that this is as good as it gets. We adjust to a life out of balance, and we excuse the discomforts, setbacks, and even the enslavement it causes us.

How to Read This Book

After I wrote *Real Solutions for Ordering Your Private Life,* I got some rich feedback. I discovered that as people plowed through the chapters, many began to feel overwhelmed. So many lists. So much advice. They felt agitated.

What are you going to ask me to change next, Lori?!

I listened to the feedback. This new book is based on the same foundational truths, but the lists are fewer, shorter, and more fun. When I give advice, it stems from the wisdom of those who have demonstrated that balance is both desirable and possible. I share from personal examples to encourage you in the race toward balance at its best.

Having said that, I know you will get bogged down at times, especially if there is so much to change in your life. When I start talking about solitude in Chapter 2 or exercise in Chapter 3, you may be tempted to lay the book aside and forget the whole thing.

Please don't!

I suggest you digest the book's contents the same way they're divided into chapters: in chunks based on major areas of our lives. Read a chapter, jot down your answers to the questions I put at the end (this is called your Balance Journal, which I'll explain later), and then take a few days—even weeks—to get a hold on the concepts you're putting into practice. Then move on to the next chapter. You'll be well on your way to a balanced life by the end of the book.

What Is a Balanced Life?

Consider these snapshots of people's lives. Can you relate?

The president of the printing company where Charlie works shares the year's profits by giving Christmas bonuses. Charlie is an industrious worker: He comes in early and stays until the job is done, however late that may be. When he opens his bonus envelope and sees the check for $500 he is thrilled. With the cost of the car repair and the leaking water heater, he can certainly use the money. But when he realizes that everyone else got the same amount he did, his pleasure quickly fades. No one works as hard as he does. "If I had more time, I'd start my own business," Charlie says for the hundredth time. "Then I could reap the rewards of my efforts and long hours. If I only had the time..."

Paula's aerobics class has ended, and she is pooped. "Hi!" a classmate calls out to her. "Want to come downstairs for a quick game of racquetball?" Paula musters every bit of energy she has left to smile and say, "Not today, thanks." She would be in better shape if she came to the gym on a more regular basis. Yet how can she? Her kids and job take every moment of the day.

Sunday dinner at Mom and Dad's house. Monday night football. Tuesday computer class. Wednesday with the kids. Thursday, Friday, Saturday—every day is spoken for. She'd love to volunteer at the homeless shelter, but right now her schedule is just too tight.

What is a balanced life, anyway? Is it merely a question of finding time to move to a more satisfying business, to improve your health, or to attend a Bible study? Is it setting goals to be accomplished just as soon as the kids finish school, the wedding is over, you pay for that great summer vacation, or the holidays are past? Is it putting your life on hold until some future, more quiet time?

Well, I can tell you right now what a balanced life is *not*. It is not merely a matter of having more time. You have twenty-four hours in a day right now, and that is all you will ever have. None of us is given the gift of more time. Neither is a balanced life a perfect life. As long as we live in this world, that is something that is out of reach. Finally, a balanced life is not a life that is permanently *set*. No, a balanced life is always fluctuating.

Okay, you may be thinking, *so what is a balanced life?*

First of all, a balanced life is a life that is ordered by the Spirit of God, one in which His Spirit has transformed the heart by grace. From this foundation comes the strength and wisdom to live a life in which all facets honor God. A balanced life, then, is a life that is well-ordered, driven by priorities and perspectives centered on Christ.

Your life is not a pie to be cut into equal pieces and conscientiously dished out to your job, your family, your church, and so forth; rather, balance starts at the center and reaches out into the spiritual, physical, emotional, mental, and relational aspects of your life. The key to a well-ordered life is to find that center.

Why Are Our Lives So Out of Balance?

In our society we are evaluated by our performance rather than by the quality of our "being." So, to placate those around us, we do what we think will satisfy and impress them, and, because we cannot do everything, we put aside those things that others don't consider to be all that important.

> **Imbalance comes from the notion that what we do determines who we are. In reality, who we are determines the effectiveness of what we do.**

Practically everyone, it seems, complains about not having enough time. No wonder there are so many recent books out on the subject of time management. People insist:

"I feel guilty if I take time for myself. It seems so selfish."

"It does me no good to set down goals. I just don't have the time to stick to them."

"My boss or others will just interrupt my plans with their have-to's, so anything I'd want to do gets crowded out."

"I don't know what's missing in my life, but I know something is."

"I know I spend a lot of time at work, but if I don't I'm afraid my income will drop. We couldn't manage on any less."

"The problem with church is that it takes up too much time. Once you start going, they want you to become involved. I just don't have time for that."

Is it any wonder that our lives are so out of balance?

Balance Is Driven by Priorities and Perspective

Balance, you see, is much more than simple time management. Balance in your personal life is determined not so much by how you spend your time, but by whether or not you let your priorities make that determination. Although this sounds easy enough, far too many people don't practice it. In fact, it has been suggested that the very worst mistake people make in time management is that they spend their time on concerns that are not their true priorities. The point is to balance what is good against what is better, and then to balance what is better against what is best.

> **The good is the enemy of the best.**
>
> —Voltaire
> *"La Bégueule" 1772*

If you are like most people in our society, you will find that television, videos, and the Internet account for a big chunk of your time. A 2006 study revealed that Americans watch an average of 4 hours and 35 minutes of TV a day—up 36 minutes from ten years before.[2] That translates to more than *nine years* in front of "the tube" in a lifetime! If you were trying to prioritize your life, what would you do? Trim the nonessentials!

Let's use our TV time as an example of what we're talking about. How can we deal with this issue? I have a few favorite programs I like to watch, but I don't want TV to hog my time. Here are some possible options:

1. Go ahead and enjoy watching TV. For some people, it is quite relaxing. Instead of feeling guilty, I set a sensible time limit, and then give myself permission to sit back and enjoy it. But I have to be disciplined. I'm careful not to go over my self-imposed time limit.

2. Double up. I do something else while watching: ride a stationary bike, write letters, file papers, or fold laundry.

3. Be selective. I record my favorite shows and specials and watch them later, skipping the commercials. This cuts my TV time to just a few hours a week.

4. Pull the plug. Sometimes I've done the radical thing: I would turn the TV off for seven days and see what would happen to my schedule. I was amazed how much time I had gained for reading and intelligent conversation.

One of the managers I work with removed all the sets from his house except for one which he kept in his basement. Now hardly any programs are watched in his household—and he has teenagers! And he himself has not watched TV in over five years.

The Spiritual Angle

I'm writing this book so anyone can benefit from the truths I learned—truths I learned through study, watching the examples of those in history, but mostly through the "School of Hard Knocks." What I found to be the best source of balance, of finding joy and purpose, is the Bible. I want to share with you from this most primary of sources, the Scriptures, so you can know the foundation on which these truths are laid. All other books, all other stories, all other anecdotes that I include in these pages are designed just to drive home the biblical principles that have helped bring order to my life.

The Apostle Paul tells us, "Now the Lord is the Spirit, and where the Spirit of the Lord is, there is freedom. And we, who with unveiled faces all reflect the Lord's glory, are being transformed into His likeness with ever increasing glory, which comes from the Lord, who is the Spirit."[3]

The very first thing Paul does in these verses is to remind the Corinthian Christians who they are! They are people with unveiled faces. They are unique and different. God loves them, and He makes them very special.

You can never hope to achieve a well-ordered life unless you begin to see yourself through God's eyes. When you are hit with a barrage of negative criticism, tricked by lies, or shaken by circumstances, only His perspective of you will keep you on an even keel. So, here they are, straight from the Source—positive truths about you.

Anytime you're feeling down, doubtful, or discouraged, repeat these concepts to yourself (I've put the Scripture references beside each one so you can meditate more deeply on them as you look them up in the Bible):

I have peace with God (Romans 5:1)

I am accepted by God (Ephesians 1)

I am a child of God (John 1:12)

I am filled by the Holy Spirit (1 Corinthians 2:12)

I have access to God's wisdom (James 1:5)

I am helped by God (Hebrews 4:16)

I am reconciled to God (Romans 5:11)

I have no condemnation (Romans 8:1)

I am justified (Romans 5:1)

I have God's righteousness (2 Corinthians 5:21 and Romans 5:19)

I am God's representative (2 Corinthians 5:20)

I am completely forgiven (Colossians 1:14)

I am sustained by God (Philippians 4:19)

I am tenderly loved (Jeremiah 31:3)

I am the aroma of Christ to God (2 Corinthians 2:15)

I am a temple of God (1 Corinthians 3:16)

I am blameless and beyond reproach (Colossians 1:22)

Believers are God's people, unique and special. Let us never forget our significance. God created you to be the very best you can be. Experience the freedom of being that person. Appreciate your uniqueness. Experience God's love and truly enjoy who you are. If you can come to see yourself this way, you won't have to prove your worth to anyone, including yourself. When you fail, this truth will give you the energy and the courage to dust yourself off and start over again.

> **Your value and identity do not come from what you do, but from who you are in Christ.**

If you are going to go the distance, begin with an understanding of who you are by establishing that relationship with Jesus, and never forget it.

True Priorities

You cannot trust that your balance will be driven by your own priorities unless you are aware of what your priorities are. So we're going to list them. Some are goal-driven (something you want to accomplish within a certain time frame—like paying your bills on time) while others are principle-driven (they indicate a quality that can't really be measured—like honesty). For now, don't worry about whether your priority list is goal- or principle-driven, measurable or even right for you. I will help you "prioritize your priorities" in a moment.

To come up with your list, consider: What is important to you? What do you know is bigger in your life that should take precedence over the littler things—things that suffer the most if you procrastinate or relationships that suffer if you neglect them? List those things here:

1._____

2._____

3._____

4._____

5._____

6._____

Now let's look at your list more closely. It's important to note that many people have two priority lists:

their true priorities

their "should" priorities

Most are hesitant to admit to themselves or to others what they truly want. Instead, they work on what they believe *should* be their priorities. The problem is, when we hold both false and true priorities, the natural result is stress and confusion. This is hardly the thing to help us achieve balance!

With that in mind, look back over your list and do some evaluation. Did you list only true priorities, or did some "should" priorities slip onto your list? If you suspect so, ask yourself who it is that you want to please. Is it . . .

> your parents?
>
> other family members?
>
> friends and neighbors?
>
> society?
>
> people in your church?
>
> people at work?
>
> someone else?

Go back over your list and put a check mark beside any items you suspect are "should" priorities rather than true priorities.

Are there some priorities you need to rewrite? If so, take time to do that now.

In the space below, list in order of priority the ones you consider to be your true top three:

1._____

2._____

3._____

Congratulations! You have taken an important first step. How are you going to stick to these priorities? Here is my suggestion, in four steps:

Step #1: Hang your list of priorities somewhere where you cannot help but see it every morning. (The bathroom mirror is a great place.)

Step #2: Read over your list every morning, renewing your commitment to your priorities each time.

Step #3: Ask yourself: "What can I do today that will help me achieve my top priority?"

Step #4: Be sure to do that thing.

I encourage you to be deliberate in putting your priorities in place because, as you well know, other influences can quickly take over. If you keep to your priorities, very soon you will start noticing that your life is revolving around what is "best," and not just what is "good" for you.

From My Heart to Yours

My parents are my most enduring, influential role models. My dad, Gerald Marvel, was a pastor throughout my whole life. When I was elementary age, he'd take me aside and mentor me on how not to lose an audience when speaking to a congregation. Maybe he was just rehearsing these concepts for his own benefit, or maybe he just wanted to include me in his grown-up world as a speaker, but I got a lot out of what he taught me. No one is better at storytelling than my dad, weaving God's truths in such a way to make them come alive and apply to today. He is a man of passion for prayer, memorizing the Word, reading voraciously, leading with integrity, and counseling wisely. I've patterned much of my life and ambition on the example my godly dad set for us.

Little did our family expect that my dad, busy with all the cares of pastoring, would end up in a mental hospital. He had a total emotional shutdown. "Are you ashamed of me, Lori?" he asked sadly when I flew to Portland, Oregon to be with my parents. There in Room 105 of the hospital I was trying to be an "agent of comfort," but was mostly seething with uncontrollable emotions. "Lori, I just couldn't do it anymore. I was doing all the reading, praying, preaching, memorizing, counseling, all the weddings and baptisms—my system just shut down. I'm sorry." Not knowing where to channel my anger, I turned on my mom. "How could you do this? Dad sheds a few tears and you put him in a straitjacket," I exaggerated. My husband Kurt pointed out that of all the people who loved and stood by my dad, it was my mom who had enough guts to do what needed to be done: admitting him to the hospital.

> **Close scrutiny will show that most "crisis situations" are opportunities to either advance or stay where you are.**
> **—Dr. Maxwell Maltz[4]**

It's easy for us to write off those who go through this kind of difficult experience. Ah, they're just weak, they haven't prayed enough, they just need to read the Bible more. Yes, it's easy to write someone off—until it's your own dad, who *did* pray enough, *did* read his Bible enough. In that hospital room, the psychologist, Dr. Dave Agnor, looked at each of us in the family, my mom, my two brothers, then at me. "Let's go in the hallway, Lori. I have something I need to share with you." Puzzled by this, I complied. Dr. Agnor looked me straight in the eye, "Lori, you're made of the same stuff your dad is, more than anyone in your family. I hear you want to win the whole world for Christ in your lifetime." "Well, yes," I admitted, afraid to hear what he was going to say next. "Take ten years off your dad's age, and that's how old you can expect to be when *you* shut down like he did." That hit me.

Dr. Agnor laid out a plan for both my dad and me to follow so we could get and stay healthy. I'd like to pass along his simple plan to you, too.

1. Make wise choices in eating.

2. Drink eight glasses of water a day.

3. Get sufficient sleep.

4. Exercise 20 minutes a day at least three times a week.

5. Take a multivitamin or other supplement daily.

Now this didn't come from some dusty theological textbook. I can't quote you chapter and verse to back up this simple plan. But I know my dad created new habits that included this advice to restore his physical body, and eventually he was able to return to his church to pastor there for another 15 years before retiring. He even ministered in Africa with Mom for a year. Today he leads with greater sensitivity and patience than I've ever known before.

Don't get me wrong. The restoration of my dad was much more than a set of new bodily habits. Watching him over these last years, I've come to see we need to nurture all aspects of our being.

Most of us today run in the fast lane of life. There are many different reasons why we choose this lane. Yet it is here that we absolutely must pause and examine the bulky weight of constant busyness that comes with running in the fast lane. The fact is, we are going to have difficulty finishing our race if we continue at the speed at which we are running. If we are going to persevere, then we must learn to run a balanced race. This will require spiritual nourishment; physical, mental, and emotional health; and balance in our various relationships, from family to church to work, and everywhere in between. Busyness must be countered with rest, comfort, and refreshment.

I'd like to say I've always followed Dr. Agnor's advice as well as my dad did. But I didn't always. Years after his ordeal, I found myself unable to get up out of bed. Kurt noticed I was on the brink of exhaustion. "Come on, I'm getting you a plane ticket so you can visit your parents," he decided. "Now they need to be agents of comfort for you." When my parents picked me up at the Portland airport, Dad didn't drive straight home. He took a detour to show me that ominous institution called a mental hospital one last time. "Don't end up in this place, Lori," he warned.

No, I won't. I still have the passion and enthusiasm I've always had. But I also maintain an eternal perspective by listening to God for any necessary correction or awesome adventure He has in store for me today. Let me share with you my two rock-bottom reminders and my three basic axioms for achieving balance in life.

First the reminders:

Rock-Bottom reminder #1: The One Good Thing Rule

This is a great thing to make a part of your daily life: Every day, in every area of your life, find the one good thing.

One time when my husband Kurt and I were youth leaders, we were on a bus bringing a group of kids back home to Phoenix from Los Angeles. Wouldn't you know it? Our bus broke down in the middle of the desert! The kids were baking in the summertime heat, with no air conditioning. We had started out on this trip with so much enthusiasm, but now here we were and there was not a scrap of that enthusiasm left. The kids were irritated with us, angry at the situation, and increasingly bickering with each other. My husband was frustrated and growing more upset by the minute.

Now I don't like negative thinking. So while my husband was outside in the blazing heat, trying to fix the engine, I stood up in the bus and said, "Guys, I just want to say something to you. Negative thinking drains us of our creative power. It drains us of spiritual well-being. So here's what we're going to do. We're going to find the one good thing in this situation. Yes, right now. Each one of you is to think of one good thing about being stranded in the desert in a broken-down bus."

Needless to say, they weren't very excited about my idea. To say they gave me negative looks is putting it kindly. So I said, "I'm serious here, guys. Every one of you is going to have to come up with one good thing." Then I started down the rows. It was really hard for them to get started, but once they did, it became quite humorous. They said things like:

"Well, at least none of us is hurt."

"We won't get in an accident if we're not moving."

"We're better off than Kurt 'cuz he's out in the hot sun and we're not."

"We're learning patience."

"We're not freezing!"

By the time my husband got back on the bus, the whole climate had changed. It was still baking hot, but now everyone was having a good time. He looked at me in amazement and asked, "What happened to these kids?" "Simple!" I said. "They found the one good thing."

Those kids had gained a sense of perspective on their situation, and with that perspective came a real sense of balance.

You say you can't find one good thing in your situation? I know it may not be easy to get started. The good thing was not easy to come by in that hot bus, either. But pause a minute. Ask God to show you the redeeming factor right where you are.

Once you find that one good thing, say it out loud. Yes, even if you are all alone. We need to hear ourselves say, "You know what, Lord? I found the one good thing here. It is . . ."

Rock-Bottom Reminder #2: Each day, determine something for which to be thankful

The companion to reminder #1 is to identify one thing each day that is worthy of your gratitude. Again, speak it out loud: "Dear Lord, today I want to thank you for . . ."

Each day, in any and every situation, make these two rules an automatic part of your life. Speak aloud those things that are true, honorable, right, pure, lovely, admirable, excellent, or praiseworthy. After all, these are the things about which Paul tells us to think.[5] When you think about these things, you're going to have a balance to your mentality, a balance in your emotions, and a balance in your perspective. That, right there, is a redeeming factor.

Now, the axioms:

Axiom #1: Find the positive in each situation

If you can find the positive in every situation you face, your most negative feelings will be replaced with a sense of joy and laughter that can bring a calmness to a heavy-laden heart, even one that is working through extremely difficult things. You say you doubt that it's possible to see anything positive in your current situation? Don't be so sure. Take a look at the cross of Jesus Christ. As Jesus' followers watched Him suffer that most pathetic, disgusting of deaths, they must have thought, *There can be nothing positive in this!* Yet God knew otherwise. Three days later, He showed them the positive in all its magnificent glory: Jesus Christ, risen from the grave! Jesus Christ, Redeemer of humanity! Jesus Christ, Savior of the world. Talk about finding a positive in a negative situation!

If you are a child of God, you have every reason to think positively. In fact, a positive perspective should be your regular outlook on life.

Axiom #2: Discover one thing to laugh about each day

Did you know that you will be much more likely to solve a problem if you take time for something fun and delightful before you go on to that problem? You were created for laughter! God Himself created it. He is a God of hope, love, and joy—and, yes, of laughter too.

We need to let go and not take ourselves so seriously. When Kurt and I moved to Phoenix, I went to a work-out gym. I walked in and these guys were making grunting noises, cussing, hitting each other. Talk about a negative feeling! There sure was one in that gym. I thought, "Lord, we've got to do something here."

I walked over to the bench press, where smelly, sweating guys were chanting, "Be the weight! Be the weight!" Then, as they lifted the weights, they grunted, "Huh! Huh! Hoo! Hoo!"

So I got in there and grabbed a bar that had no weights. I lay back and gave two loud exhales, then chanted, "I gotta be the weight! I gotta be the weight! I gotta be the weight! Ooohaaah! Ooohaaah! Ooohaaah!"

Let me tell you, every guy in the gym stopped and stared at me. Well, I was brand new. I didn't know anybody, so there was no reason to be embarrassed. I wiped my face and exclaimed, "Whew! Oh, hi, men."

One guy walked over and stood in front of me, glowering. "Hey lady, what's your problem?" he started. "This place is serious! We don't goof around here! We don't laugh! We don't cry! We don't do our nails! We're serious about pumping iron in here!"

I stood up, "You want to know what your problem is?" I asked. Everyone's attention was riveted on me. "This is not a hospital," I continued. "This is not work. It's a gym. Recreation. Fun. Exercise. Joy. Get it? You guys come in here and spit and slap and cuss like it's some disgusting place. Now, I'm new to the gym" (as if that weren't perfectly obvious). "My goal is to bench my weight. And when I do it, I want there to be whooping and hollering and whistling and clapping, and cheering—lots of cheering. Do I make myself perfectly clear?"

I went back the next day. I sat down and put five pounds on each side of the bar. As I did this, one guy came over and said, "Oh, you need to breathe out when you push it up . . . but we're having fun! We're having fun!" So I did a couple more. And more the next day, and the next day, and the next. It took me several months, but I kept working. As I worked, some of the guys would go by and say, "Just be the weight. Just be the weight. You breathed out when you pushed up; be the weight." Then they would add, "Guys, we're having fun."

Others would chime in: "We're having fun—be the weight, be the weight." In this way they would help me.

After a year of regular workouts at the gym, I awoke one morning and told my husband, "Kurt, I'm gonna bench-press my weight today."

I walked into the gym. I didn't say anything to the friends I had made; I just picked out my weight and sat down. Suddenly one guy called out, "Whoa! Whoa! Guys! Everyone! I think the mama is gonna do her weight!" Then he looked straight at me and said, "Ma'am, if I'm not mistaken—is this your weight?"

I said, "Maybe."

"Yep, it is! Guys!" he called. So everybody stopped and gathered around.

"Hey, you don't have to do this," I said.

"No, no!" they replied. "We had our orders. We know what to do."

I said meekly, "I have no idea if I can even do it." Yet I lay back and got ready.

"Remember. Breathe out. Be the weight, and get it off your chest," one guy said. "Just give it all you've got. But we're having a good time—having a good time!"

So I got under the weight. (Grunting, panting, groaning.) It was a lot of weight to bench. (More grunting, panting, groaning.) But I made it!

"Wooh! Wooh! Wooooooh! Wooh!" The guys yelled. They slapped each other and shouted, "Good job! Good job!"

Then the first guy came over and said, "Umm . . . What makes you so different, lady? Last year this place was nothing but a death trap. Then in walks this chick who tells us we're not allowed to spit, cuss, and yip. That we have to laugh, whoop and holler, slap each other, and high-five. What happened?"

"I tell you what happened," I said. "I have a God who has a playful spirit. He's full of joy. He's full of life. He's full of laughter. He's full of hope. It's just the way Christians live, and I shared it with you."

I know that some personalities have a more difficult time laughing than others. I realize some people just don't see things in a very humorous light. Yet, ask the Lord for little moments of humor, and pause from your busy day to laugh. Just watch what lightness and balance will come about!

Axiom #3: Look forward to one thing each week

Every week, find something you can look forward to. It might be nothing more that going to the library and reading a good book, or watching a ball game on TV. It might be calling up a friend and saying, "Let's go out for hot chai." If you're married, it might be something as great as a big date with your spouse.

One time Kurt picked me up at the airport after a long trip. I was exhausted. He said, "Lori, we have a date night tonight."

I said, "Kurt, no. Not tonight. I'm really too tired."

"Nope," he said. "You're going to go home, take a shower; and put on something nice. Then we're going out."

I knew perfectly well that this was all my fault; I had "trained" him this way. I had always told him, "Why don't you sometimes think up a date? We'll just do it!" Well, now he'd thought one up and I didn't want to do it. So I sighed and complained as I dressed quickly and not that well. Then I walked out the door and there stood a white limousine. The driver stepped up, opened the door; and said, "Madame, your date has hired me to take the two of you to dinner."

I had never been in a limousine before! I grabbed the driver and gave him a big, big hug, all the time jumping up and down and exclaiming, "Oooooooh!" The driver just shook his head and said, "You don't get out much, do you?"

Well, we got into that limousine and I was all energy. I helped myself to the soda pop they had in there; I turned all the lights on; I opened the sky roof.

"I see you got your energy back," Kurt said.

"Oh, of course I got my energy back!" I said. "Take me out to dinner!"

I told him I didn't care where he took me. Any old hamburger place would be fine. We could just whip out a white tablecloth and a candle and it would be great. People would walk in, look at us, and say, "Oh, isn't that... uh... different?" and I would tell them, "It's the thing I looked forward to all week!"

Most of my one-thing-per-weeks are not as magnificent as a limo ride, but whether gigantic or small, I eagerly look forward to each of them.

> **The choices we make every hour of every day create our future.**

Balance Journal

Reading is fine, but to get the greatest benefit, it is important to process the information you read and then to make it your own. To help you do this, at the end of each chapter I will make suggestions for things you might want to jot down in a Balance Journal. You may want to get a notebook and keep it just for this purpose. In the next chapter I will introduce you to my spiritual director, Gail MacDonald. Gail has stressed the importance of journaling—an area in which I admit I still need to grow. I've always found journaling a chore, but I recognize the wisdom of journaling when it comes to reflecting later on the thoughts God wants to impress on us. So I have made the Balance Journal less of a chore, I believe, by keeping suggestions brief, to the point, and often a lot of fun.

Here is the Balance Journal assignment for this chapter:

> In your journal, copy down the three top priorities that you came up with earlier in this chapter.
>
> What are some actions you can take to help you achieve these major goals or live by these high-priority principles?
>
> What might be some of the obstacles to you accomplishing them?

Keep your Balance Journal with you as you go through this book. The more you write in it, the more of a valuable tool it will become as you look at the areas of your life that need more balance. You will see a pattern emerge of how God is at work in you to fulfill your destiny. Before you go on to each new chapter, I suggest you re-read what you have written to prepare you for the next step.

Now we will begin the balancing act with Spiritual Balance.

Chapter 2

Spiritual Balance

For a day in Thy courts is better than a thousand outside. I would rather stand at the threshold of the house
of my God, than dwell in the tents of wickedness.[6]

Is there anything that draws us into spiritual balance more than
the Psalms? I don't think so. The quote above is from Psalm 84,
and it's very typical of the praise and adoration we see throughout the Psalms. We also see lament and fear, discouragement
and doubt. Yet through it all, David, the greatest of the
psalmists, triumphantly states that if he had his choice between
one single day in God's presence or a thousand among those
who do not honor God, it would be no contest at all. The one
day in God's presence would win, hands down. Now that is
spiritual balance!

A Sense of God's Spirit

Can we ever hope to maintain a sense of God's Spirit in this
chaotic, unpredictable world? Only if we make a definite,
concentrated effort to do so. It won't just happen, that's for
sure. If we rely on external structures to provide continuity and
security in our day-to-day living, we're going to be in trouble,
because the external structures of our lives often go through
complete changes. Therefore, we must have the inner strength

to handle whatever circumstances or external structures may alter in our lives.

But, some insist, *I sense God's Spirit in me by the ways in which He uses me.*

This is great, but there is one very important thing we must understand: God works *in* us before He works *through* us.

> **It can't happen through you until it happens to you.**
> **—Lloyd John Ogilvie**

Spiritual balance means yielding ourselves completely to God and resting in Him. To help you do this, consider this psalm—a glowing testimony to the security of those who put their trust in the provision and safety of God:

> He who dwells in the shelter of the Most High
> will rest in the shadow of the Almighty.
> I will say of the Lord, "He is my refuge and my fortress,
> my God, in whom I trust."[7]

Do you want a sense of God's Spirit? Then dwell in the shadow of the Most High. Rest in His presence. Claim Him as your refuge and your fortress. Now that is real peace.

Yet, this is not easy to do in our culture. We are in such a mode of producing and doing that we have forgotten the importance of *being.* The fact is, however, our *being* must precede our *doing.* Only then will we have the maturity to lean back and receive God's best from His merciful hands.

> The unweaned child is at its mother's breast for what it wants—milk. The weaned child, however, is content to rest in its loving mother's arms and receive whatever she desires to give.
>
> —M. Robert Mulholland Jr.
> *Invitation to a Journey*[8]

Whenever Jesus went through Bethany, He stopped to see His good friends Mary and Martha. They were always happy to see their Lord. One day when He arrived Mary rushed to sit at His feet, eager to listen to all that He had to say. Martha knew that He would be spending the night, so she rushed around to make everything perfect for His stay. And of course there was dinner to make. Finally, as she paused to wipe her face and brush the hair out of her eyes, a thought occurred to her: How come she was doing all the work while her sister was sitting and enjoying their company? She stomped into the front room and announced, "Lord, don't you care that my sister has left me to do everything by myself? Tell her to help me!"

"Martha, Martha," Jesus answered patiently. "You are worried and upset about so many things, but only one thing is really important. Mary has chosen what is better; and it will not be taken away from her."

Hmmm. That tells us something, doesn't it? If we are not careful, we, like Martha, can allow constant busyness to crowd out the gold and silver that could have been part of our lives. If we are to run the race well, we absolutely must make it a priority to withdraw and replenish ourselves spiritually, emotionally, and physically. We cannot allow our busyness to get us so out of balance that we fall down exhausted at the end of the race—or perhaps before it is even over. Sure, there is a great deal that has to be done in this life. Yet God wants us to do all that we do in His name and to His glory. The only way we can do that is to come to Him regularly for the spiritual rest, refreshment, and guidance we need to run our race well.

> The times I've overworked and made myself and everyone else miserable, it's been because I needed people's appreciation, or their pity, or their admiration too much. I was trying to prove I was worth something by my hard work . . . But when service becomes a pain, or a means of personal gain, then the service needs to be curtailed for the sake of the higher good of resting in Christ's presence. God called you to be His beloved, not His beast of burden.
>
> —Frank Barker
> "The Martha Syndrome"[9]

How can we gain the inner strength we need to run the race well? The only way I know is to spend time with God each day. Before you start listing all the reasons why this just won't work for you, let me hasten to say that I understand that a person's particular station in life may require that he or she use some creativity in developing spiritual disciplines. Certainly a spiritually balanced life looks different for each of these individuals:

- the mother of infant twins
- the parent of a rebellious teenager

- a busy student
- a retired person
- a single person
- someone staggering in the wake of a tragedy
- the CEO of a large corporation

Time with the Lord, sitting at His feet in worship, doesn't need to take a specific amount of time. It doesn't have to happen at a particular hour or place, and it need not have a distinct format.

Let me tell you about Colin, the seven-year-old son of friends of ours. He and his mom were riding with my husband Kurt and me one afternoon. Kurt and Colin's mom were having a deep discussion, and Colin was looking at me with an engrossed look.

"Colin," I said, "what are you thinking?"

"Miss Lori," Colin said, "I was just wondering, do you ever have two-second conversations with God?"

"Two-second conversations with God?" I asked. "What do you mean, Colin?"

"Well, sometimes, all of a sudden, I have a two-second conversation where God just speaks to me and then, boom! He's gone. It's like just in a moment," Colin said. "I can hear His voice, and I can tell He's right there. And I just wondered, does that ever happen to you? Do you have two-second conversations with God?"

I looked at that little boy and I realized that God's Spirit was speaking to him. "Colin," I said, "do you know what? I used to have those two-second conversations with God, just like you. And I, too, would sense His presence intensely."

Colin looked straight at me and said, "How come you don't anymore?"

"Well, I guess I'm too busy doing other things, like preparing talks and meeting with people and writing papers for my doctorate," I explained lamely. Then, after a moment, I added, "I'm afraid I'm so busy, and I've cluttered up my life so much, that I can't hear those two-second conversations anymore."

Colin was perplexed. "Miss Lori," he asked, "why would you want to write a paper or talk to people when you can hear God for two seconds?" I was silent, but Colin continued to press. "Why do you think I can still hear Him, but you can't?"

"Colin," I said, "it's because you're fresh from God. And you don't have things in your life that clutter it up. You have the ability to sense God's presence in the simple moments of life. I've crowded those things out."

After that conversation, I took the matter to God in my prayer time. I repented for no longer having those moments of intense awareness of His presence. I thanked Him for allowing a little seven-year-old boy to remind me that those moments are more precious than anything I can ever do or encounter.

I truly believe that it is in seeing the humor in life, and in rediscovering simple pleasures, that we discover why we were created. We can be in Christ, and be aware of His presence, even in the midst of all the different things going on in our lives, if we just train our senses to become aware of Him.

> The fruit of prayer is a deepening of faith.
> And the fruit of faith is love.
> And the fruit of love is service.
>
> But to be able to pray we need silence
>   silence of the heart.
> The soul needs time to go away and pray
>   to use the mouth
>   to use the eyes
>   to use the whole body.
> And if we don't have that silence
>   then we don't know how to pray.
>
> —Mother Teresa
> *Words to Love by*[10]

Spiritual Rest

Some of the lessons we learn in life come wrapped in emotions, situations, and choices that are extremely difficult to endure. But not all life's lessons come through hard times. Some come to us through joy and rest and answered prayer.

The early Church father Augustine did have a rough time of it, but it was his wayward spirit that got him in trouble. He spent his early years blinded by arrogance while pursuing a life of lust and hedonism. His believing mother Monica prayed for him relentlessly and even followed the young man around trying to redirect his restless spirit. Finally, Augustine went through a twofold conversion—first intellectually as he sought to rid his life of false doctrine. Then he went through a spiritual conversion as he picked up the letters of Paul and read convicting words about the outcome of a sinful life. With a heart of anguish, he surrendered himself to the mercy of God. As he wrote his famous *Confessions* at the turn of the fifth century, Augustine was overwhelmed by God's wisdom and grace as he remembered his own life of sin. He began the work with a burst of praise that sounds like one of the Psalms of David:

> You arouse us so that praising you may bring us joy, because you have made us and drawn us to yourself, and our heart is unquiet until it rests in you.[11]

The young Augustine had discovered God as his source of spiritual rest. You just have to learn to rest in Him.

> **We need rest from our guilt, doubt, confusion, emptiness, dryness, and despair. We long for the peace of God that transcends all understanding.**
>
> **—Dr. Siang-Yang Tan**
> *Rest*[12]

We all know how vital physical rest is to the body. Even more important is to discover the spiritual rest that Augustine found. Why is it then, that so many of us miss out on it? This is especially perplexing when we realize how many of us long for it in the deepest part of our beings. Spiritual rest from God includes Sabbath rest, in which we take a break and rest from our work just as God rested from His.

Towards the end of Paul's letter to the church in Philippi, he writes: "Do not be anxious about anything, but in everything, by prayer and petition, with thanksgiving, present your requests to God. And the peace of God, which transcends all understanding, will guard your hearts and minds in Christ Jesus."[13]

This is the essence of spiritual rest.

Solitude and Silence

I could talk separately about the value of taking time to be silent, to quiet our hearts and minds. But I want to focus on solitude—for silence is often a major ingredient in our times of solitude.

What do I mean by solitude? Simply put, it is spending time alone with God. To seek solitude is to deliberately withdraw from all human contact or interaction for the sole purpose of meeting with our Lord. Is it hard? You bet it is. Most of us are surrounded by people and noise and jobs that need to be done ASAP. Yet solitude is an important spiritual discipline. If cultivated and nurtured, it yields a great bounty. It frees us from things, from the opinions of people, from the values and evaluations of those around us. Through solitude we take time to listen to God's opinion of us—and He will take that opportunity to reassure us of our true identity. He will woo us like His beloved. Is that too feminine of a picture for you? Then consider how He will cradle you like a father holds his young child. Too childish of a picture for you? Get over it! He loves you—and by taking time alone with Him, you allow yourself to receive His love. You will learn to trust and rely on Him as you never have before.

> Without solitude it is virtually impossible to live a spiritual life.
>
> —Henry Nouwen

How might you spend a time of solitude? Here is a suggestion: Take a silent prayer sabbatical. Because it is so vital to focus on praying, I'd like to suggest prayer days and prayer retreats, times when you get away for four to six hours to be alone and pray. You may be able to get away for a day and a night, or maybe two days or even an entire weekend. Spend part of the time praising God, waiting before Him, confessing your sins, and reading God's Word. But most of all spend the time in prayer. Take walks. Ride your mountain bike. Sit in the sun. Sit on the grass under the shade of a tree. The point is to be alone with the Lord. I am big on studying the Scriptures and memorizing God's Word, but this is not the time or place for these endeavors. This is the time to listen. E. Stanley Jones had what he called his "listening post," a certain fence post where he would go to simply stand and listen. Unless we designate a place and time to listen, we are sure to spend most of our time talking or doing.

Just stand and listen? you may be asking. *Listen to what?*

To God. I suggest you ask directly: *"Lord, what are you saying to me?"* You see, God is constantly speaking to us. The question is not whether there is anything to listen to. It is whether we are actively listening and in tune to what He is saying.

Here is where silence and solitude comes in. Listening takes place during these times. It happens in quietness, when we are separated from the things that would otherwise take our attention. Granted, we can have moments of solitude in the midst of our hectic schedules, but there should be a place and a time for us simply to withdraw. Jesus is our ultimate example, and that is exactly what He did. Take a fair amount of time, be silent before God, and ask Him, "Lord, what are you saying to me?"

A man once approached Mother Teresa and said, "I don't sense God's presence in my life."

"There are two things you can do that will bring God's presence back to your life." She told him. "Number one, spend an hour a day praising His character, just praising who and what God is. Number two, stop doing what displeases Him." Then she looked straight at the man and said, "If you will do those two things over a period of time—stop doing what you know displeases God, and spend an hour a day adoring His character—His presence will return to you in fullness, through Jesus Christ."

I firmly believe that sometimes we need to do exactly this. There are things we are intentionally doing that block God's grace and presence in our lives. Spending time adoring Him will help to correct that imbalance.

When we go into solitude, our primary motivation should not be to plead with God for help. Too many of our prayers run this way: "God, help me. God, do this for me. God, do that for my friend or my family." There is nothing wrong with presenting our petitions to our Heavenly Father. We are commanded to do so. Yet, our times of solitude should be spent listening and loving. This will bring the balance that is so sorely missing in our lives—and, I might add, in our society and our churches as well!

> **Truly I have set my soul in silence and in peace, like a weaned child at its mother's breast.**
>
> **—Psalm 131:2**

Getting Started

I can relate to Gordon MacDonald's first attempts at practicing these forgotten Christian disciplines:

> Silence and solitude have not come easily to me at all. I once equated them with laziness, inaction, and unproductivity. The minute I was alone, my mind exploded with a list of things I should do; phone calls to make, papers I should be filing, books unread, sermons unprepared, and people I ought to see. . . .
>
> But concentrating even when there was silence became desperately difficult. I learned that I had to warm up, to accept the fact that for about fifteen minutes my mind would do everything it could to resist the solitude. So among the things I did was to start by reading or writing on the subject of my spiritual pursuits. Slowly, it seemed, my conscious mind got the message; we (my mind and I) were going to worship and meditate, and the sooner the mind got in touch with the inner garden on the matter, the better it would be.[14]

Here are some guidelines to help you as you get started practicing solitude and silence:

- Schedule times to be alone with the Lord each day (Don't worry about the length of that scheduled time right now—it is far better to plan for ten minutes and really do it than to set the lofty goal of one hour and be sporadic about it)

- Periodically set aside an hour for silence, then try to work up to two hours

- Listen to God more than you speak to Him—this works well with relationships with other people, too!

- Begin planning for a day-long retreat where you can be alone with God in solitude and silence

Christian Fellowship

Another necessary discipline to develop spiritual balance is Christian fellowship. This means gathering together with other believers for the purpose of worshipping God. It may be in a church congregation or it may be in a small group, such as a home Bible study. Taken a step farther, it also includes serving and caring for one another, praying and reading Scripture together, and reaching out to the world in the love of Christ.

The Christian life should be filled with joy and celebration, but for too many it is more of a chore, or it leads to guilty feelings because it seems nothing is being accomplished. Why is this so? One big reason is that we try to do everything alone: we pray alone, we read the Bible alone, we carry our own burdens, and we reach out a helping hand all by ourselves. We live our Christian lives independently rather than linked together with other believers. This means we cannot easily share one another's joys and successes, nor can we adequately comfort others in their sorrow and pain. We don't experience the support that real Christian fellowship should bring, and we are unable to use our spiritual gifts as God intends us to use them.

True Christian fellowship not only allows us to be there for others who need us, but also draws out a willingness in us to ask for and to receive help when we need it. It also calls us to be more honest, transparent, and vulnerable with one another.

Realize your Ministry

Each of us has a ministry. God has chosen us to accomplish His mission in this world. We are His agents here, His method of operating. We are His vessels. I love this truth: "All this is from God, who reconciled us to himself through Christ and gave us the ministry of reconciliation."[15] Did you get that? God has literally entrusted us with the message of reconciliation! We are ambassadors, allowing God to make His appeal through us. What an awesome privilege!

Yet, this means we must be good stewards of this privilege, for it is also a responsibility. We must not give up. We must not lose heart.

> **Without us, He will not; and without Him, we cannot.**

A number of years ago, when I visited the country of Jordan, I went to see the ancient site of Petra. In order to get to that rock fortress, we had to go by horseback along a trail lined with 750-foot-high rock walls. Each person on that tour had a horse and a personal Arab guide. I leaned forward on my horse and said to my guide, "Sir, my name is Lori. What is yours?"

"Mohammed," he answered.

Now I'm not known for being shy! And when I see an opportunity to share my faith, I do. I believe we're to be winsome in our sharing, but we are to share nonetheless. "Always be prepared to give an answer to everyone who asks you to give the reason for the hope that you have," the Apostle Peter admonishes us, and adds, "But do this with gentleness and respect."[16]

So I said, "Mohammed, do you know that Jesus Christ loves you? And do you know that He died on the cross for you?" I made a cross with my fingers.

Mohammed looked up at me and said, "Sorry, no speak English."

I prayed, *God, how can I communicate Your love to him in a way he'll understand?* And God brought an idea to my mind: *Sing him a song.*

"Mohammed," I said, "I'm going to teach you a song."

"No, Lori!" he exclaimed. "No, no, no, no!"

I didn't pay any attention to his objections. I leaned up on the horse and said, "It goes like this . . ." Then I sang,

> God is so good.
>
> God is so good.
>
> God is so good,
>
> He's so good to me.

"Now Mohammed," I said, "I want you to repeat after me."

He said, "No sing, Lori. Please, no sing!"

"Mohammed," I said, "you can either sing it with me or I'll sing it louder."

"Okay, okay. Shhhh! Don't sing it louder! I sing, I sing!"

So we sang through the song, with me singing a line and Mohammed, slowly and very off-key, copying it. After each line

I enthusiastically exclaimed, "That's great, Mohammed! That's just great!"

When we finished, Mohammed said, "Lori, let us sing together!" I agreed, and with a loud voice (and still off-key) he sang, "God is so good..." and because we were between two cliffs, his voice echoed, "Good, good, good, good."

His friends, who were leading the other people, looked at me accusingly and insisted, "What are you doing to our friend?"

Yet Mohammed kept right on singing: "God is so good (good, good, good, good)," over and over again, accompanied by my tongue-in-cheek warning, "Mohammed, shhhhh! Not so loud!"

Finally, we got to the rock fortress, and Mohammed said to me, "Lori, bring all your friends around. I want to sing them a song."

"Come here, you guys," I called to the group. "My guide would like to sing a song for you."

We gathered all the people around. Mohammed stood up on a little box he had found, looked at me and said, "Start me off, Lori. Like one, two. One, two, three."

I started him off, and he picked it up—off-key, of course:

> God is so good.
>
> God is so good.
>
> God is so good.
>
> He's so good to me.

Our whole group cheered and clapped, and Mohammed stood there with a huge smile on his face. He looked at me and said, "Lori, I am a good singer!"

After everyone left, I said, "Yes, Mohammed, you are a good singer. But did you know that God loves you? He died on the cross and wants to give you life."

"Lori, I do not know about that," Mohammed said, "but I do know this . . ."—and he opened his mouth to sing again.

"No! Okay, okay, Mohammed, I know what you know!"

He got on his horse and rode off. As I watched him go, I said to the Lord, "Please, God, will You use that song in his life someday when he's questioning the purpose and the meaning of his existence? Bring back to his mind the fact that You're so good, so good to him."

We must each find the ministry God has for us, then be willing to overcome every barrier thrown before us to be faithful to that ministry. A life lived for oneself can never be a truly balanced life.

> **You have a ministry. However insignificant it may seem to you, it is very significant to God.**

To have a spiritually balanced life, we must combine our times of solitude and silent worship with times of joyful Christian fellowship and group worship. The focus is not to be on us, but on God and service to others.

Spiritual Directors

Every young believer needs someone who has walked this way before and is willing to reach out and lend a guiding hand. In my book, *When Roosters Crow: A Fresh Approach to Christian*

Accountability, I discuss in depth about surrounding ourselves with "roosters"—people who can stand with us, pray with us, ask us the hard questions, and sometimes crow like a rooster when our soul is in danger. Think of the rooster crowing that dark night when Peter denied he knew Jesus. The rooster brought Peter face to face with himself, his sin, and his Savior.

We need accountability—male "roosters" if you're a man; female ones if you're a woman. I get kidded a lot for having female "roosters." All I can say is, they're not clucking hens! If you ask God to help you build a team of "roosters," He'll honor that request. It's in His interest to give you the "wake-up calls" you need to stay on track in your spiritual journey.

My roosters, nine in all at the moment, find themselves in various life stations. But each and every one of them (Becky, Charlotte, Connie, Ginger, Ida, Lisa, Martha, Michelle, and Penny) makes a great contribution to my life. We meet monthly, encouraging each other in the faith, discussing the pitfalls we're aware of, memorizing Scripture together as well as practicing the other spiritual disciplines I mention in this book. We begin the year's commitment together with a retreat. It's a fun way to get to know each other better, but it also lays a great foundation of commitment to God and to each other. It's a huge sacrifice of time for each of us.

Why do it? What's so important about having a deliberate, committed group of people in my life? As busy as I am, how could I ever justify spending all that time with these sisters? My answer to that is simple: How could I ever live *without* having roosters?

> The Church is meant to be a community of spiritual friends and spiritual directors who journey together to God. We must become that community. Prayer is the starting point.
>
> —Larry Crabb
> *The Safest Place on Earth*[17]

My rooster experience—is it mentoring? Is it coaching? Counseling? Accountability? There are a lot of buzz words today to describe relationships people have that are intended to improve someone's life. Basically, we're talking about the relationship Paul had in the first century with his protégé, Timothy. I'm going to add another term to the mix: Spiritual Director. Let me explain the differences among all these terms.

Mentorship

A mentor helps someone become proficient in a skill or competency. You can mentor someone in the area of time management, for example. You can be mentored in person, or just by reading someone's books. Reading biographies of exemplary people in history is a great way to be mentored. Reading about Winston Churchill and Mary Slessor, for example, has helped me grow in the area of leadership, and in seeking God's calling and direction for my life.

Young people contact me from time to time asking me to mentor them to become a skillful public speaker. I weed out the serious from the casual by telling them this: "After you've read my books and listened to my presentations on CD, come back and we'll talk about me being your mentor." Most inquirers drop like flies after this—but then along comes a young woman like Jennifer Adzima. Jennifer was honored as Focus on the Family's "Brio Girl" in 2005-2006. She wrote advice articles to teenage girls for *Brio* magazine and was a spokesperson for wholesome living among her peers. She heard me speak at a Senior High School Leadership Conference in Los Angeles. When I asked her to read all my books and listen to all my tapes, she didn't hesitate one bit, but ordered them that same day. Later on, she interned at our Celebrate Life International office in Acworth, Georgia, for a summer. I was able to speak into her life through my own example, by the example of our CLI staff, and by directly training her in the area of public speaking. A year later, Jennifer was the youth breakout speaker at one of my *Wild Women of God*° conferences.[18] This was true mentorship.

Coaching

When you think of coaching, sports like soccer or track come to mind. But coaching can include mental as well as physical training, and not have anything to do with sports. It is goal oriented. You hire a coach to discipline you through a regimen that will take you further than you thought possible. Coaching expert Tony Stoltzfus points out that "[n]othing is more empowering, nothing causes us to reach higher and accomplish greater things than having people in our lives that love us for who we are and believe unconditionally in what we can become."[19] Stoltzfus defines coaching as "a relationship centered on helping people discover and fulfill their destiny, which uses goals and action steps to move strategically toward that end."[20]

Counseling

What picture comes to you when you hear the word "counseling"? Perhaps lying on a couch relating how you wet your bed as a child while a bespectacled psychiatrist takes notes and mumbles "um-hum"? Or does it drum up images of an advice giver telling you what's wrong with you and what you should do to change? Maybe you have a positive memory of a pastoral counselor listening through your difficult situation and offering thoughtful advice on how to weather the storms of life. Whatever the picture, whatever your experience, counseling involves a look at the root causes of one's problems and presents the counselee with choices on how to improve the situation.

Counseling, like other forms of help listed here, involves one person as the counselor, and usually limits the counselees to one person, a couple or a small group. The aim is to fix a problem and as Stoltzfus reminds us, to help the client become whole emotionally and psychologically.[21] When the client reaches this wholeness, or the crisis has been worked out, the counseling is over.

Accountability

Do you need to break free from addictive behavior? Do false beliefs or destructive thoughts rule your life? You need an accountability partner. My roosters—and my husband—meet that need in my life. When temptation comes our way, we need someone we can confide in, someone who won't let us off the hook. It's "tough love." Accountability only works when you want it. It would be pretty easy to lie to an accountability partner. But you're only fooling yourself if you do. God puts friends and partners in our lives for our benefit. Take advantage of it by being totally honest with your accountability partner.

Pastoring

I love my pastor. Kurt and I attend a large church in Woodstock, Georgia, outside Atlanta. Pastor Johnny Hunt has a gift of making you feel that you have his full attention, that you're the only one in the room—even though there may be dozens of people waiting to have a word with him. Pastor Johnny fulfills his role as pastor much like a shepherd tends sheep. In fact, pastors are often referred to as the shepherd of their flock. The word "pastor" has at its root the concept of tending, keeping, putting to pasture, feeding, and guarding sheep. Of course we're talking about people, not sheep, so pastoring refers to tending to the spiritual needs of a congregation. It's a one-to-many relationship. I recognize in my pastor that he has a calling to lead the congregation in the ways of God's truth, and Pastor Johnny is quick to point out that God holds pastors accountable for this.

Spiritual Directors

Okay, a spiritual director is much like a mentor—you're in an intentional relationship with a director much like you'd be with a mentor. Spiritual directors coach you in that they push you to levels you didn't think possible. Often they listen and advise, much like a counselor. They certainly dish out large doses of tough love, like an accountability partner, and they look after the spiritual care of people like a pastor. But here's what makes spiritual directing special:

- The focus is on your spiritual growth—it's all about who you are becoming rather than on a skill you need to master

- The emphasis is on spiritual maturity, even though a director may touch on the physical as well as other aspects of your life

- As spiritual direction expert Reverend Rebecca Langer points out, "Spiritual direction is not goal-oriented but God-oriented"[22]

- A spiritual director gives you assignments designed to help you go deeper and to stay deep in your walk with God

- A spiritual director is not your peer, but someone further along in spiritual maturity, someone you could "sit at the feet of" and benefit from their life

- A spiritual director is in a special one-to-one relationship with the "directee"; the director isn't a shepherd to everyone in a congregation the way a pastor is

Author James Emery White clarifies:

> Spiritual directors will listen to us, help us to respond to God with greater freedom, point us to practical disciplines of spiritual growth, love us and pray for us. He or she is not a counselor, therapist, guru or dictator, but a mature Christ follower who helps us discover the movement of the Holy Spirit in our life.[23]

Finding a Spiritual Director

Now that we've defined the terms a little, I want to share with you how I've benefited from spiritual direction.

A number of years ago, I led a breakout session while speaking at "Praise Gathering," sponsored by song writers/artists Bill and

Gloria Gaither. Gail MacDonald attended the elective seminar where I spoke on a Balanced Life. After the session, Gail approached me and said she liked my presentation. "I could be passionate about what you were talking about," she stated. She gave me her business card.

My first impression was that she was calm, not flashy, but purposeful and deliberate. I didn't know her, but I loved her husband's books. Gordon MacDonald's works, which are many, spoke to me on many levels. I refer often to his teaching on Sabbath Rest and other disciplines of the faith.

I tucked Gail's business card away for future contact. In the meantime, I had already been asking God to show me who could mentor me on a deeper level in the spiritual aspects of my life. In my mind I was looking for someone wiser than I whom I could call my spiritual director. I was already "interviewing" women to see if there was a "chemistry" there. I didn't tell them I was looking for a spiritual director. Here's how I would conduct the "interview." I'd ask three questions:

- What are you encouraged by when you see my life?

- What would you caution me about?

- What else would you like to say to me?

Based on their answers, I'd get a pretty clear idea whether they were serious about my spiritual growth and whether they could address my blind spots with counsel beyond where I was. I wasn't looking for someone who was perfect—or I'd still be looking until I die! But I was looking for someone who demonstrated a well-ordered life, had weathered life's storms and had rich truths to share from experience. I was not in a hurry to find such a woman. I was content to ask the Lord to reveal such a person.

A few weeks after meeting Gail MacDonald, I gave her a call from my cell phone while I was out doing errands. After asking her if this was a good time to talk, I asked my three questions. I was not prepared for the responses Gail would give me. In just a few minutes, she impacted me with insights, truths, convictions, and wisdom that I couldn't just keep in my head. I was scrambling in my car for napkins, gum wrappers—anything to take notes on so I could remember what Gail said. In that single phone call, she was doing what White talked about, which was to help me discover the movement of the Holy Spirit in my life. I was deeply moved and humbled by this conversation—then I tucked those note scraps away as material I knew the Lord wanted me to work on later.

One year later—yes, a year later!—I contacted Gail again. We had talked during that year, but this time I called with a specific request: "Gail, would you prayerfully consider being my spiritual director?"

Her answer took me aback. "Lori, I've been waiting for you to ask me that." Gail knew I had to initiate this relationship. She waited a whole year for me to come around and see it was God's will. I don't think I procrastinated by waiting a year. I was being sensitive to God's Spirit to prepare me for this level of intentional relationship, and to lead me to Gail.

Now two-and-a-half years later, Gail has pumped more spiritual life into me than I thought was possible. Here's her style of directing:

- She asks questions rather than gives advice
- She encourages me to journal—in my case this means we meet, I take notes, type up those notes and email them back to Gail—a great way to see whether I listened to her

- She meets with me one-on-one, not in a group setting

- She often gets Gordon's perspective on a matter

- She confronts graciously but tenaciously, again, through the use of pointed questions, not finger pointing

- She puts together quotes, lists of reading material and other resources for me to ponder—and then follows up with questions about them

- She emails with me, and then in preparation for a meeting, she'll go back and read all our old emails

- She prays for me

Why Have a Spiritual Director?

Here is an obvious statement: "You don't know what you don't know." We all have blind spots. We need spiritual direction by someone who can see those blind spots. And we need to muster the courage to ask what those blind spots are. Without that kind of correction and direction in our lives, we're going to be destined for mediocrity. I don't know about you, but mediocrity is a dirty word to me! How sad it would be to live your whole life and discover that you've been shallow, unchallenged, undisciplined, and finally, without purpose. Much as it strains us to grow, isn't it better to take calculated risks, challenge ourselves to improve, and discipline ourselves to live with excellence in all things? I don't want to die with any regrets. Listening to my spiritual director is how I safeguard against mediocrity and regret.

Can't I just have Jesus as my spiritual director? you might ask. Of course, Jesus is our ultimate director in all areas of our lives. His Word provides the best advice. But I dare say you *won't* consistently let Christ direct you without another, more mature human being, asking you pointed questions that direct you straight to Christ and His Word.

What if my director points out something I have a hard time hearing or that I may disagree with? Good question! We won't always see eye to eye with our spiritual director, and that's a good thing. During one visit with Gail MacDonald, the subject of my appearance came up. I told Gail that some men have been giving me unsolicited attention lately. "I was minding my own business at a restaurant, just on my way to the restroom," I related, "when a guy leans back in his chair and says, 'Smelling good and looking hot!'" *Was that directed at me?* I wondered. Yes it was. I ignored the man and made a beeline to the ladies' room. I asked Gail what might be happening that I've been getting this kind of male attention (I also talked with Kurt about it earlier). I was eager to know how she might direct me spiritually to handle this.

"What have you been doing to bring this attention to yourself?" Gail queried.

I was miffed. "Nothing!" I declared with a touch of defensiveness.

She probed further, "Do you know how men are aroused?"

"Visual stimulation, yes, yes, I know," I interrupted.

"What were you wearing?" Gail was not backing down, and I felt myself getting hotter under the collar.

"I was wearing a skirt and top—something I'd wear anywhere."

"How short?"

"The skirt? Up to here," I pointed above my knees. "Gail, God doesn't want us to be frumpy! And Kurt approves of what I wear."

Gail very wisely turned the conversation to include the bigger picture. It was more than a choice of clothing or perfume. We discussed my energetic personality, and even my persona on stage as I speak. Gail encouraged me to take this home and talk about it with Kurt and to pray. "Obviously this is striking a nerve with you—go find out what's behind it all."

Later, when I did talk with my husband about my visit with Gail and her comments that set me on edge, he asked somewhat tongue-in-cheek, "Do you need to 'fire' your spiritual director?" He recognized that I could find someone that I could always agree with, or I could live with the fact that I'm sometimes going to disagree with my director.

Well, I didn't "fire" Gail. I'm very thankful for our relationship. God did show me some things about myself through this encounter with Gail on my personality, appearance, and persona. She pointed me to the Holy Spirit, and as I listened to Him, a joy came over me that I am purposefully created by Him for His glory. Gail compliments me on how focused I am to listen to what she has to say, but she's also quick to point out that I don't substitute her for the Holy Spirit. I'll take what people say to me and bring it to my prayer time. *Jesus, what are YOU saying to me through this?* will often be my prayer. Then it's *His* voice I set out to obey unconditionally.

As a result of this discussion, I am now more aware of what I wear. I do not want to cause anyone to stumble. And I'm more aware of how my personality comes across to people. We all have a personality style; we all have strengths. The problem comes when we ignore the pitfalls that accompany those strengths, or when we resent the counsel of those who are looking out for our best. In the end, even if you choose not to go the route laid out by your spiritual director, there is a nugget of truth to be mined. If you approach your director's comments with an attitude of humility, you'll grasp that nugget of truth—and you'll be better off because of it.

Become a Spiritual Director

Another reason it's important to *have* a spiritual director is because God may want you to *be* a spiritual director for someone else. Christians are never to retire. Sure, you may stop taking a paycheck for work you do, but we're never to get to the point where we think we can just "slide into home." The moment we stop growing is the day we start dying. God isn't finished with you here until He takes you to be with Him. Maybe one of your jobs in your "golden years" is to provide that direction to someone younger than you. You don't even have to wait until you're old to be a spiritual director. There are always newer believers who would love to have your counsel. Make yourself available to God for this. He'll guide you in His timing, just like He did with Gail MacDonald and me.

How to Find a Spiritual Director

Are you convinced you'd like to find (or become) a spiritual director? Here are some tips on finding one:

- Ask God to direct this process
- Find someone who is mature, competent in spiritual counsel, and available

- Find someone you would want to become like spiritually—even though you may have little in common in other ways

- Don't look for someone you'd always agree with—consider someone outside your Christian denomination who truly loves Jesus Christ and might be able to shed light on your own traditions

- Ask God for both the courage and the humility it takes to initiate this relationship with someone

- Be patient—it may take some months or over a year to establish this committed relationship

- Count the financial cost—there may be travel and lodging costs, books to buy, etc.—don't be taken by surprise, but budget for it

- Set up the relationship in such a way that works for both of you—long-term and short-term relationships with a spiritual director are possible[24]

- As the directee, you are responsible to make the meetings happen, and to take to heart what the director says to you

- Listen, listen, listen!

- Do the homework that the director assigns you

- Have a definite ending date for this relationship—then use that date as a time to evaluate whether to continue for another season together

I have dedicated quite a few pages to the topic of Spiritual Directors. I hope you'll take to heart the need for this kind of directing. Let's move on now to another important ingredient if we're to have balance in our spiritual lives: Servanthood.

An Attitude of Servanthood

An attitude of servanthood enables us, by the power of the Holy Spirit, to submit to the Lord and serve Him by serving others with humility and joy. When we have the right kind of servant attitude, we will not be easily offended by cynical, critical people, or upset when the ones we serve don't appreciate us. When it comes right down to it, the Lord is the only one we serve. So, what difference do the praises and affirmations of people make? That's not to say we don't appreciate and enjoy support and encouragement of others. Of course we do. Yet in true servanthood we can live and serve without it. The Lord's affirmation is enough.

Certainly one aspect of servanthood is developing a meaningful volunteer life, giving out with nothing tangible coming back in return. This might be done under the auspices of a Christian organization, but it doesn't have to be. To do something that takes time and effort on our part and expect nothing in return adds a sense of purpose and meaning to our lives.

When I was seventeen, I got my driver's license. All I could think of was driving- anywhere, anytime. So I said to my mom, "I'd like to use our car."

"Well, Lori," Mom said, "you're new with your license. You can't just go out and drive the city. You have to have a reason."

"Well, uh, I do have a reason," I said.

"Oh? And what is it?"

"Umm, well," I stammered, "I'm going to go visit ... the nursing home."

My mom said, "Okay, that warrants the car."

So I got out the phone book and looked up "Nursing Home." I jotted down an address, got in the VW, and went to a nearby nursing home in Vancouver, Washington. I walked in, went to the desk, and said to the nurses there, "My name is Lori Marvel" (that's what it was at the time), "and I'm seventeen years old. I wanted to get out and use the car so I told my parents I was going to come and visit your nursing home. I have just an hour, and I was wondering if you could give me the name of someone who never has anyone to visit him or her."

The nurses looked at each other. Then one said, "Well, welcome to our home. You can visit anyone here. They don't have visitors—maybe a couple—but most of them have none. We're not the high class nursing home that most people put their parents in."

"So I can just go into a room and visit?" I asked.

"That's right," the nurse said.

I went into the first room I saw, and there was a lady lying in bed. "Hi!" I said. "I just wanted to come in and meet you and talk a while. Can you tell me about your day?"

She stared at me. "Ummmm," she said. Then, "Do you want money?"

"No," I said, "I don't want money. I just wanted to make a new friend. My name is Lori and I wanted to use the car, so I decided to come and talk with you. What is your name?"

"Mrs. Smith," she said. Then, "Honey, how much do you charge to visit me?"

"No, no, Mrs. Smith," I said. "I don't want any money."

"Are you taking a survey?"

"No!" I said. "I'm seventeen years old, and . . . you know what? I really need a new friend. So I'm wondering if you'd be my friend."

"You're sure you don't want any money?"

"Positive."

"Well, then, I'll tell you about me," Mrs. Smith said. "I used to be a schoolteacher. Back then, we'd have all the kids in one room, and I'd teach . . ." She started telling me her story. It was wonderful.

Finally, I interrupted her to say, "I have to go now, Mrs. Smith, but I just wanted to tell you—I really am enjoying having you for my new friend."

"Little one," she said, "when you leave, would you do me a favor?"

"Sure," I said.

"Would you get one foot outside of my door and one foot inside my room, and as loud as you can, say, "Good-bye, Mrs. Smith! I love you! I'll come back and see you again!'

You don't really have to come back and see me, Sweetheart. But won't you just say it anyway for me?"

"Why do you want me to do that?" I asked.

"Oh, Sweetheart, because you're my first visitor in so long. And I haven't heard anybody tell me that they love me and would want to come back to see me. And I'd just . . . I'd like to hear it. And I want everyone else to hear it, too."

So I got halfway out in the hallway, halfway in the room, and I said in a loud voice, "Good-bye, Mrs. Smith! I love you! I'll come back and see you again!"

"Louder, child, louder!" Mrs. Smith said.

"GOOD-BYE, MRS. SMITH! I LOVE YOU! I'LL COME BACK AND SEE YOU AGAIN!"

I wept all the way home. Through the rest of my high school years, every Tuesday and Thursday I was in that nursing home, going from room to room. God began to teach me that in life I had to give out, not wanting anything in return.

You might want to go to a nursing home, or you may prefer to volunteer somewhere else. Here are some ideas to consider:

> Volunteer to take care of someone's kids and give the parents a night off.
>
> Volunteer to mentor an at-risk teen in a public school or juvenile court setting.[25]
>
> Get some friends together and clean up a roadway (or a park or a beach).
>
> Help out in a school classroom. There are many ways to make yourself useful there, from making photocopies to grading papers to helping a child with his or her home-work to sharing your own personal expertise with a classroom.
>
> If you're good at home repairs, offer to help older people and those who can't afford to hire the work done.
>
> Go ahead and visit a nursing home once in a while. You never know, you might be there yourself one day.

You may think of something completely different. Fine. But whatever you decide to do, do it faithfully and develop a meaningful volunteer life. Giving when you get nothing tangible in return will add a special dimension of balance to your life.

I never look at the masses as my responsibility.

I look at the individual. I can love only one person at a time. I can feed only one person at a time.

Just one, one, one.

You get closer to Christ by coming closer to each other. As Jesus said, "Whatever you do to the least of my brethren, you do to me."

So you begin . . . . I begin.

I picked up one person—

maybe if I didn't pick up that one person I wouldn't have picked up 42,000.

The whole work is only a drop in the ocean. But if I didn't put the drop in, the ocean would be one drop less.

—Mother Teresa
Words to Love by[26]

Once you are working toward balance in your spiritual life, you will be ready to move on to balancing your physical life.

Balance Journal

It's time for your Balance Journal again. Did you enjoy writing in it in the last chapter? I hope so. I intend the journal to be fun, yet thought-provoking. It can also reveal some deep-seated emotions you weren't expecting to raise to the surface. If journaling bogs you down, as it sometimes does me, just answer those questions that are the most meaningful to you. You're doing this for you, not anyone else. I'd rather you jotted down a couple of phrases than get overwhelmed and not use this tool at all. It's like my workout at the gym in Phoenix. You're going to sweat and experience some pain, but there is also much gain—and you can have some fun in the process!

Entitle this section of your journal *Spiritual Balance*. Write down your thoughts on the following questions:

How do I react to the daily ups and downs in my life?

How could I react in a healthier way?

How might I be more serene?

Put a check beside the things in the following list that you might add to your life. When could you start or accomplish them? Give yourself a "due date."

- ☐ Set aside time for prayer every day.

- ☐ Study a book of the Bible with a friend (if you're not already in a Bible study—some people do too many Bible studies and neglect other areas of their lives!).

- ☐ Make a list of uplifting and thought-provoking books you want to read.

- ☐ Begin to plan toward going away on a spiritual retreat.

- ☐ Find a spiritual director (just get the process started; remember, it could take many months).

- ☐ Consider becoming a spiritual director (list people you have a burden for concerning their spiritual development—are you available?).

Here's one you could do right now to end this time in your journal today: Read David's prayer in Psalm 27:4-8 and write down one phrase from it that means a lot to you.

Chapter 3

Physical Balance

Throughout my life, people have always told me how they think I should act. I have heard it all:

"Lori, don't be so dramatic."

"Don't talk to strangers, Lori."

"Lori, you need to cross-stitch, knit, and have babies instead of climbing mountains, riding bikes, and going parachuting."

"Lori, you talk too much. Try and be more like a lady."

As a young woman, I was even sent to two different charm schools. Neither one took. When I tried to be all the things people told me I should be, I felt as if I were in a straitjacket. Then one day I realized something important: *God did not create me to be all those things.* So I burst out of all the constraints, and I have never regretted it for a minute.

That's not to say I don't see room for improvement. I certainly do. Yet I want to make those improvements in keeping with who God created me to be. God has His own perspective of me, and that's the only perspective that matters. Not everybody likes me, but that's okay. There's only one Lori Salierno in this universe (*Thank goodness for that!* you may be thinking), and I am going to be the best Lori Salierno I can be.

Being the best I can be starts with remembering that my body is a temple of God. I don't dare let it get run down, shabby, lumpy, or weak. That's the reason this chapter is so important to me.

Let's talk about the things that will keep our bodies—God's temple—appropriate places for Him to reside. Let's talk about eating well, exercising, getting a sufficient amount of rest, and minding our appearance. But first, let's talk about habits.

Habits: The 21-Day Challenge

In 1960, Dr. Maxwell Maltz published a self-help book that took the nation by storm for several decades. His scientific research led him to some simple, yet profound principles that changed lives. I bet your local library has a yellowing copy of this paperback, *Psycho-Cybernetics*.

A cosmetic surgeon by trade, Dr. Maltz was amazed that some of his facial reconstruction patients, after undergoing a wonderful change to their outward appearance, still thought of themselves as "ugly" or as having a "freakish" feature.[27] He discovered that a transformation on the outside didn't always translate into an improved self-image. His book walks the reader through practical exercises to imagine oneself as creative and accomplished, happy, empowered, youthful—a winner. He asks the reader to bear with his exercises, without judgment, for 21 days. Maltz writes:

> It usually requires a minimum of about 21 days to effect any perceptible change in a mental image. Following plastic surgery it takes about 21 days for the average patient to get used to his new face. When an arm or leg is amputated the "phantom limb" persists for about 21 days. People must live in a new house for about three

weeks before it begins to "seem like home." These, and many other commonly observed phenomena tend to show that it requires a minimum of about 21 days for an old mental image to dissolve and a new one to jell.[28]

Dr. Maxwell Maltz may have popularized the 21-day formula for developing a new habit, but I first heard about this in my psychology classes in seminary. Is it really 21 days? Not 20 or 22 or 100? In my experience, I have seen new patterns solidify after about 21 days, but I'm not legalistic about it. When I speak on the subject in my presentations, I just say, "If it doesn't stick with me after 21 days, I just begin another 21 days!" With some of my habits, such as Scripture memorization, I just keep it up, and now it's been 21 *years!* You can keep it up, too.

In my speaking career, I get invited to present on healthy habits for school assemblies. One time I was invited to speak to an inner-city student body where they hadn't had an assembly for 17 years. Why? Because the last time they tried, a riot broke out! But they asked me to come anyway and to talk about healthy values. It was the most hostile crowd I'd ever witnessed at a school. As I stood up to speak, one girl shouted out, "Hey lady, take this!" and thrust her middle finger at me. From another bleacher, a guy piped in, "Whatcha doing after the assembly, 'cuz my two friends and I wanna 'do' ya!" *Why did these young people hate me so much?* I wondered. They didn't even know me well enough to hate me. There was something deeper going on, something faulty in their belief system. These students needed to "dehypnotize their false beliefs," as Dr. Maltz would say.

I proceeded with the assembly, and God gave me a strategy to grab the students' attention and make a big impact that day. All I had to do was talk about truth, integrity, self-control—and even virginity. You could see the hunger on the kids' faces. When I mentioned the "V-word," however, you'd think I'd poured acid on these students. Virginity was a dirty word to them. Funny, I thought it was just the opposite.

I share this story with you because I left that assembly with a heart broken for young people everywhere who don't know right from wrong. How could I convince them of the truth about how they were created so they could change their lives? That was when the Lord inspired me to start a nonprofit organization dedicated to building character in young people by introducing them—perhaps for the first time—to absolute truth and practical leadership skills. This nonprofit is a reality today: Celebrate Life International. We are thriving in many settings as we bring these truths—what we call Universal Principles—in a life-changing way to youth.

Those principles that young people (and adults!) need to adopt in their lives developed into a philosophy that we call *Teach One to Lead One*.[29] The *Teach One to Lead One* program emphasizes the importance of developing new habits. Our experience with youth confirms Dr. Maltz's findings that it takes about 21 days to break an old habit and to replace it with a healthy habit. Something changes in the brain during those days, a new pattern develops that enables the habit to "stick" for the long haul.

Of course it may still be easy to stop practicing your new habit once formed. But you'll notice that you're making a deliberate choice to go back to laziness—the habit *was* beginning to take shape. Now you just have to decide to keep walking in the truths you're learning.

Now let's apply the principle of the 21-day challenge to balance in your physical life. In the sections ahead, I share ways you can improve your physical health, appearance, restfulness, and energy. Just like Dr. Maltz requested of his patients, I ask you "reserve judgment" and develop new habits. "Perform the exercises," Dr. Maltz appeals, "even if they seem impractical to you. Persist in playing your new role...even if the new self-image feels a little uncomfortable or 'unnatural.'"[30]

Eat Right

Let me guess. Being the busy person you are, more nights than you intend you end up at a fast-food place, ordering hamburgers. You're overweight, but, hey, who isn't? Exercise? Please! It's all you can do to drag yourself home at night. Prepare a nutritious meal from scratch? Are you kidding? You're tired at night, but between finishing up office work and doing the endless jobs that need to be done at home (did someone say "honey-do list"?), you are lucky to be able to plop down in front of the television with a microwaveable pizza before nine or ten o'clock—and it takes a bit of TV watching and a pint of ice cream for you to unwind enough to sleep.

Am I at least partly right? I thought so!

Well, let's talk about your upkeep of the temple God has entrusted to you, and let's start with what you put into it to keep it going. That's right—food.

Most of us know that a nutritious, well-balanced diet is important, especially when we're under stress. We also know that eating the wrong things will cause us to gain weight, and that too much weight is unhealthy. In fact, the majority of us have at one time or another tried to follow a weight-loss program. We all have seen the pictures of the stick-thin models in magazines and catalogs that are supposed to represent the ideal body shape. So what is the answer? Dieting? Ugh!

Actually, as many of us know by experience, diets that restrict your intake of calories seldom work. What dieting does do is lower the rate at which your body burns calories. That's because your body automatically goes into starvation mode. It thinks it's dying, and since it desperately wants to survive, it slows down and burns calories at a much slower rate than normal. It seems strange, but if we want to burn fat we have to take in enough quality calories to give our bodies the energy to do the fat-burning work.

Instead of thinking *diet*, think *lifestyle*. The way to get your body at its peak is to embrace balance in your life. Change the way you eat. Learn what is healthful, and then apply what you have learned. Not only will your body change in positive ways now, but your new habits will make those changes a part of you for the rest of you life.

> **The only diet that really works is the one you can stick to for the rest of your life.**

When it comes to weight, be realistic. To compare yourself to a fashion model or a man on the cover of *GQ* magazine is unrealistic (not to mention downright dangerous) for the vast majority of us. To want to look 35 when you are 55 is unrealistic. To hope to be tall and slender when your parents and grandparents are short and plump is unrealistic. To decide to lose thirty pounds before your high school reunion two months from now is unrealistic.

If you pursue an unrealistic goal, you will undoubtedly become discouraged and give up on the whole thing. It is helpful to choose a range to work within rather than a set amount. ("I want to be able to wear a smaller clothing size by the high school reunion.")

Once you reach your preferred weight, take action to prevent yourself from going back up. Refuse those excuses that will lead again to weight gain. I live by the motto that if I am brutal with five pounds now, I will never have to deal with twenty pounds later.

Healthy Nuggets

Most of us know the basic habits for healthful eating. We have seen food pyramids. We know that fast foods and sweet treats are not good for us. We have heard all about the evils of deep-fat fried foods. Yet when we are hungry and those things are calling out our names, it's awfully hard to resist. Here are some tips that will help make the battle easier:

- Keep plenty of nutritious ready-to-eat foods in your pantry and refrigerator

- Stay away from refined sugar and high-carbohydrate foods; they lead to the storage of excess fat in our bodies

- Drink lots of water, at least eight eight-ounce glasses per day[31]

- Bake, broil, or roast instead of frying—and eat this way when you go to a restaurant, too

- Never shop for groceries when you're hungry, when your willpower is at its lowest

- Eat the right foods or snacks when you're hungry and stop when you're full—even if there is food left on your plate

- Take small bites and eat slowly

- When you're dying for a "bad" snack, wait ten minutes before giving in—the desire just might pass

Fasting

I have made fasting a regular part of my life. There is a lot of information on the subject, and I have read most of it. If fasting is new to you, I'd like to suggest a couple resources to you to get you started. Then I'll focus on a few of the elements of fasting that have made the most impact in my life.

This topic of fasting could fit both in the Physical Balance section of this book as well as the Spiritual Balance chapter. Fasting affects our whole being, actually, but I chose to include it in the Physical Balance chapter because we fight the battles related to fasting most prominently in our bodies. It's a spiritual battle, but the manifestation of it is in our bodies. Then, when we experience breakthrough and joy in our fasting, it's a spiritual victory that shows itself also in our bodies in the form of peace and physical well-being. We also experience emotional balance—so it's definitely a key ingredient to our well-ordered life.

The first book I'd recommend is a classic that is enjoying a surge of new interest among readers: *Celebration of Discipline* by Richard Foster.[32] His treatment of fasting takes the subject out of being a dreary chore into one of wonder and rediscovery. He includes fasting as part of the "inward disciplines," alongside meditation, prayer, and study. Foster cautions us as we attempt to restore spiritual disciplines in our lives:

> ... to know the mechanics does not mean that we are practicing the Discipline. The Spiritual Disciplines are an inward and spiritual reality, and the inner attitude of the heart is far more crucial than the mechanics for coming into the reality of the spiritual life.[33]

Elmer Towns' book *The Beginner's Guide to Fasting* is a great place for starting out.[34] And his more recent book, *Knowing God through Fasting,* will take you deeper in your intimacy with the Lord.[35] Towns echoes some of the points I make in this book about balance. There are many reasons to fast, he says, but the best reasons have to do with coming closer to Jesus as we...

- taste the goodness of the Lord
- wait in God's presence to become like Him
- come to Jesus to enjoy His presence
- drink from God's presence to get spiritual satisfaction
- learn to discipline yourself even as Jesus did
- grow spiritually into the image of Jesus
- gain spiritual perception of God's world
- enter God's rest as you know His heart

As I incorporated fasting into my lifestyle, I noticed right away that our motivation is the most important factor if we're going to get anything from fasting. Think about toddlers having tantrums to try to get their way. They kick and scream, flop on the ground—and my favorite—threaten to hold their breath until they get what they want. Silly, isn't it? But do we sometimes approach God with religious kinds of "tantrums"—trying to get Him to do what we want? Fasting can become an elaborate tantrum if we're not careful. Why fast in the first place? What is our motivation?

The first thing to remember here is that God cannot be manipulated, so we shouldn't waste our energy trying to manipulate Him. He's not impressed with our grand show of piety.

So why fast? Fasting doesn't manipulate God, but rather, it prepares our hearts to receive God's answer to our situation. That was a huge insight to me as I took on the discipline of fasting. Do you have an overwhelming decision to make? A loved one's illness that has you perplexed? A longing in your heart to come closer to God? A feeling like your prayers are stopping at the ceiling? A major career change? These are signals for you to consider fasting.

By engaging in this discipline, you are surrendering your appetites to God for a higher purpose. It puts you in a position of humility and dependency. Once in that state, God can speak His truths to you while you are more receptive.

I was led by the Spirit to fast on a fairly regular basis. He kept nudging me to increase the number of days. I'd do a week-long fast, then ten days, then 20 days. Finally, on a couple occasions, He has provided me with the strength and commitment to complete a 40-day fast. These were focused around major changes in our nonprofit organization.

I don't share all this to be presumptuous. In fact, we're to fast in secret whenever possible. I share this as an encouragement to you that most people are physically able to fast, and if we are healthy, we can fast for longer than most of us can imagine right now. But like any other new habit, we need to take it easy at first. You could start with a "Sabbath fast" from sundown to sundown.[36] Maybe do a fast where you eliminate meat and soft drinks from your diet, or a fast where you take in nutrients in the form of juices that you make in a machine. Often the Lord has led me to do a water-only fast.

It's rare that the Lord would lead someone to go on an "absolute fast"—no food or water of any kind—for an extended period of time. Some call this a "miraculous fast" because our bodies are not designed to live longer than several days without hydration. It'd take a miracle to complete. Be careful with your zeal. Take time to listen to God for His wisdom on how long and what kind of fast you should do.

Okay, you have your major situation that warrants fasting. You've checked your motivation before the Lord and are asking Him to prepare your heart to receive His answer for your situation. You have an idea when and how long you should fast, and what type of fast it should be. Now how do you get ready? How do you actually pull it off?

> Fasting . . . was so common [in the Bible] that no one had to ask what to eat before a fast, or how to break a fast, or how to avoid dizziness while fasting—everyone already knew.
> This is not true of our generation.
>
> —Richard Foster
> *Celebration of Discipline*[37]

There are many resources on the Internet on what to eat leading up to a fast, recipes for healthy juice drinks during fasting, and how to come off of a fast.[38] But here is a quick list from my gleanings of those websites:

Before a fast

- Drink large amounts of water anytime you can

- Enjoy freshly squeezed juices each day

- Avoid animals products

- Use very little salt

- Try vegetable soup, one bowl each day (could be lunch or dinner)

- Consider fasting with others as a team, especially if you're fasting about a common concern

- If you take medications for anything, consult your doctor about your dosage during fasting, and whether you can fast at all

During the fast

- Give your feelings of hunger over to God by talking to Him about your challenges

- Talk with an experienced, trusted friend about your fasting[39]

- Keep up with your hydration and get enough rest

- Be receptive to what the Spirit of God is saying to you on any matter, including the situation that inspired you to fast in the first place

- On an extended fast, you will need to take into account the interesting changes that could take place in your body at different times: weight loss, elimination of material from the colon, pimples, and other manifestations due to your body detoxifying itself

- Just before you end the fast, prepare your body to take on solid foods—perhaps by eating small amounts of easy-to-digest foods

After the fast

- Start simply, gradually increasing the amount of raw fruits and vegetables in your diet

- Wait a few days before reintroducing meat into your diet

- Give yourself a break-in period: around one day for every three days of fasting—for a 20 day fast, the break-in period would be around 6 days

- Do you like what you see in your new weight? Consider changing your eating habits so it won't all come back on[40]

- Continue in the same prayerfulness you had during the fast, because God can be just as much a part of your eating as He was part of your fasting

- Celebrate! You have, with God's help, accomplished a spiritual discipline—what did He tell you during your fast?

Fasting, when combined with solitude and silence, is the best way I can think of to become intimate with our Heavenly Father. Now let's move on to other areas of our physical lives that can contribute to our overall balance. Let's start with exercise . . .

Make Time for Exercise

In a healthy, balanced lifestyle, exercise is indispensable. When we exercise, our bodies release endorphins, a natural substance that can give a feeling of well-being. Exercise also serves as an outlet for stress, and it sets in motion biochemical changes that speed up our bodies' ability to burn calories. Exercise builds muscles, and muscle burns more calories than fat. That means that even when we aren't actually exercising, we are still burning calories faster than before we started exercising.

So if exercise is so great, how come we don't all do it?

Because it's too hot.

Because we're too tired.

Because the kids have the sniffles, or they're cranky, or they get bored.

Because the gym's too crowded or it's too far away.

Because we're going to, but not today.

Because of any one of a thousand other reasons.

Listen to these procrastinators. Do any of them sound like you?

JACK: "I'm going to start exercising when my friend Dave does. I'm working on a project at the office right now that keeps me there late nearly every evening, but once that's done I'll try to get Dave to go with me."

It's wonderful to get encouragement from your friends and family, and it's certainly true that difficult circumstances can hinder your schedule. Yet the bottom line is that it is up to you to set aside time to start a lifetime of fitness. If your excuse is anything like Jack's, I suggest that you write down your exercise schedule on your calendar right alongside your other important appointments. Come up with a realistic schedule, and then stick to it, no matter what. Never cancel your exercise session. If you can't possibly make it at the scheduled time, reschedule it for later that day, or the next day at the latest.

RUTHANNE: "I am going to get started, but I'm down in the dumps and I feel like I may be coming down with a cold."

Unless you really are certifiably sick, this is called procrastination. When it comes time to exercise, it is the most common ailment known. Don't wait until you feel great and have the energy. You'll feel better physically and emotionally *after* the exercise routine, not before it. Getting out in the sunshine for a brisk walk for 30 minutes can take the edge off of feeling depressed, too. Just get your exercise gear on and do it!

CHRISTINE: "I tried exercising. I went to the gym every other day for three weeks, and I didn't lose a pound! It just doesn't seem to work for me."

Some people expect to see immediate weight loss and an increase in their strength and body tone after only one session. When they realize that working out requires slow, steady commitment in order to achieve any real gain, they become discouraged. Focus on rewards other than immediate weight loss, such as lowering of your stress and an improvement in your energy level.

NICK: "I don't get it. Every time I get started on an exercise routine, I injure myself and can't continue."

No wonder Nick dives headlong into a challenging new regimen and ends up overdoing it. Then, in pain, he cannot go back for so long that he gives up. If this sounds familiar, try setting more realistic goals for yourself, then pare them down a step further. So what if you leave the gym knowing you could have done more? Tomorrow you'll come back eager to push a little bit more.

Many people feel guilty or stressed because they know they *should* exercise regularly, but they just don't want to. Exercise can be strenuous and monotonous, to be sure, and when you're over your head in daily responsibilities, it's even more difficult to tie on those athletic shoes and head for workout. The secret is to develop a realistic strategy for fitting exercise into your specific lifestyle.

The benefits of regular exercise far outweigh the time, trouble, and sweat you will have to invest. Instead of thinking of the time you are spending, think about . . .

- boosting your energy
- relieving stress
- keeping your appetite in check
- creating strong muscles and bones
- strengthening your heart

- achieving better weight control

When you take all of this into consideration, regular exercise is pretty much worth it, don't you think?

Tricks to Pump You Up

Even when you find a routine that you enjoy and that works for you, there will likely be times when you feel too busy, rushed, or tired to exercise. When that happens, use these "tricks" to help pump up your motivation:

See exercise as NON-optional. The minute you allow yourself to argue about going, you increase your chances of settling into a sedentary lifestyle. Would you skip work because you couldn't think of what to wear? Would you stop brushing your teeth because you're too tired? People make time for their non-optionals. Make exercise one of yours.

Reward yourself. Get new music to listen to on your MP3 player while you exercise. Pick up a new magazine or a good book to read while you ride the exercise cycle. Treat yourself to a smoothie fruit drink (with added protein) after you finish a vigorous exercise.

Trick yourself. Tell yourself, "Today I'll work out for only fifteen minutes." You'll find that once you get going, practically every time you'll keep on until you've put in much more than your minimum time.

Use your spare moments. On the days you don't exercise, use these tried-and-true techniques for getting unplanned exercise: Park in a far corner of the parking lot so you will have to walk to and from your car. Never use an elevator if there are stairs. Do stretches and calisthenics before you go to bed.

Set realistic short-term goals. Forget that 25 pounds you need to lose. Set a goal to swim an extra lap, ride the exercise bike an extra five minutes (or raise the intensity a notch), or walk all the way to the top of the hill in your neighborhood instead of just to the corner. Do sit-ups while you watch the evening news. Then take pride in achieving those smaller goals.

Use your lunch break. Instead of eating in the lunchroom—or even worse, working through lunch—use part of the time to take a brisk walk or maybe even ride a bicycle.

"But," you may be saying, *"I hardly have any time with my family the way it is. If I start on a regular exercise program, I'll never see them."*

Good point. If you have this problem, why not exercise together with them? One man used to have his toddler daughter sit on his feet while he did sit-ups. The little girl loved this "daddy-daughter" time. Look at these other suggestions and put a check by the ones that might work for your situation:

- ☐ Walk or jog while you push a stroller.

- ☐ Ride along with your kids when they ride their bikes.

- ☐ Use an exercise bike in front of the TV when you are watching a family movie.

- ☐ Plan family outings in places where you can walk or hike.

☐ Play sports as a family (badminton, Frisbee, swimming, or bowling).

Do you not know that your body is a temple of the Holy Spirit, who is in you, whom you have received from God?

—1 Corinthians 6:19

When we consider our modern lifestyle with all its "conveniences," we notice there are things we've gotten used to that are robbing us of a quick and spontaneous way to exercise. Consider these alternatives:

- Do your own yard work

- Play active games with your kids, such as basketball, jump-rope, tag, or flag football instead of couch-potato video games

- If you *are* into video games, do the active ones that keep your body moving such as those with a foot pad for dance steps or with a controller that you swing like a bat or racquet.

- If you don't have a dog, offer to walk your neighbor's dog

- Do isometric exercises (tighten your stomach, buttocks, and thighs) while you drive

- Wash your own car

- Carry your own luggage

Need more help to stick with your exercise program? Become aware of your excuses for skipping exercise and find a solution that fits you. For instance, if at the end of a busy day you are just too tired, try exercising at lunchtime or early in the morning. It may also help to make appointments to exercise with friends. If you are accountable to someone else, it is a lot more difficult to back out at the last minute. Most importantly, if you miss a day, forgive yourself and get right back into your routine. It *will* pay off.

Exercise is one of the most worthwhile investments of time and energy that you can make, and it doesn't have to cost you a bundle. You don't need a great exercise wardrobe, state-of-the-art equipment, or a membership in an exclusive gym. All you need is a willingness to find what works best for you and a determination to keep at it. You won't be sorry!

Get Enough Rest

The frenzied activity of our busy schedules, day in and day out, leaves most of us physically drained. "Work hard and you will succeed," we are told by our society. So we allow work to dominate our lives and squeeze out other crucial needs, including rest. We even tend to play hard, so that when we finish our recreation, we are more tired than ever.

We need true physical rest, and that includes enough time not only for relaxing leisure but also for sleep. If we are to properly care for the temple that God has entrusted to each of us, we must ensure our physical rest by refusing to overwork and overschedule.

How often have you been reciting a litany of your busy, involved life and been interrupted by someone asking, "Do you ever have time to sleep?" What was your answer? Did you laugh? Did you brag about being able to get along on five hours of sleep?

Unfortunately, many of us don't put much value on sleep. That's too bad. Research shows that far too many of us aren't getting enough. According to the National Sleep Foundation, adults need between seven and nine hours a night. That's called our *basal sleep need*. Teenagers' basal sleep need is about nine hours, while preschoolers need 11 to 13 hours of sleep. On top of the basal sleep need is the *sleep debt* we accumulate by regularly not getting the basal sleep we need nightly.[41] When we have a sleep debt, it affects our ability to deal with stress and to ward off disease.

There is hope, though. Some business executives are rediscovering the lost art of sleeping eight hours—a conscious rejection of the workaholic lifestyle "enjoyed" by most executives. *Wall Street Journal* staff writer Nancy Jeffrey reports, "Sleep, that rare commodity in stressed-out America, is the new status symbol. Once derided as a wimpish failing... slumber is now being touted as the restorative companion to the creative executive mind."[42] Maybe more of us will follow the example of Robert Fulghum. He is famous for the poster, "All I really need to know I learned in kindergarten," where he reminds us how great it would be if we would all just lay down and take a nap. Amen!

Sabbath Rest

Sleep isn't the only kind of rest we need. We also need to *vacate* (vacation) and to *recreate* (recreation). Christians and Jews alike are taught to take one day a week to rest from the usual stresses and concerns of life. We often think of this break as a spiritual concern. It is, of course, but did you know that it also makes good physical sense? Getting away—really away—from our hectic schedules allows us to vacate and recreate, literally restoring our bodies.

Gordon MacDonald outlined it well in *Ordering Your Private World*:

1. Sabbath rest is a time of looking backward, of loop-closing.[43]

2. Biblical rest happens when we pause regularly amidst daily routines to sort out the truths and commitments by which we are living. You could call it a recalibration of the spirit.[44]

3. We rest by affirming our intentions to pursue a Christ-centered tomorrow. We ponder where we are headed in the coming week, month or year.[45]

So, what types of guidelines should you use for your day of Sabbath rest? First of all, make it a rule that you will do no occupational work on that day. Beyond that, make a list of those things that will give you a sense of joyful rest. Consider such things as . . .

- taking a nap
- enjoying a leisurely walk
- having a simple but tasty crock-pot meal with your family or close friends
- relaxing and doing nothing
- lying on the couch and listening to music
- reading a book

- playing a game

- sitting and talking over a cup of coffee

- reading the Bible

- doing spiritual study

If something you try is not restful to you, cross it off your list. When something else occurs to you, add it and give it a try.

When you go to bed rested and revived, you will be more able to take that experience of Sabbath rest into the week ahead.

Make the Most of What You Have

Some of us are short and some are tall. Some are skinny and others are plump. Some have big feet, straight hair (or no hair!), a big nose, or some other feature we dislike. Yet whatever our physical attributes—or drawbacks—we can make the most of what we have.

A sweet man by the name of Martin was badly burned in a fire. His face is scarred, his ears and nose are mangled, and his fingers are gone. Physically, he is hard to look at. Yet few who really know him consider him anything but attractive. To a large degree, this is because of his wonderful spirit and attitude. Yet he has also learned the secret of making the most of the body that God has entrusted to him.

You can do the same. Here are some thoughts for both men and women to get you started:

> **Take inventory of your closet.** Many men reach blindly into their clothes closet, grab the first shirt they come to, give it a sniff, and either toss it in the dirty clothes pile or put it on. Pants? They keep the pair on they wore last night! Am I exaggerating? Maybe a little.

But most men give less thought to their wardrobe than women. Guys, it's not a bad thing to look through your closet to see what still fits you, what looks good on you, what you never wear, what is moth-eaten, and what is no longer cool.

And women, we can take a rainy afternoon to sort through our closet, too. I have a policy to throw out any clothes that I haven't worn in a year. I pass them on to Goodwill or to a friend who may like them. With empty space in your closet, you'll see what you enjoy wearing and will more easily remember what you have when you shop for clothes that go with those items.

Stay up-to-date in your wardrobe and appearance. Some think it's "Christian" to be frumpy. Modesty is a virtue, but frumpy just squelches the creativity of God in your situation. Remember my conversation with Gail MacDonald on this? Find a way to be both stylish and glorifying to God!

If you don't have a knack for outfitting your business and casual attire, go shopping with someone who does. Rhonie, the wife of CLI Research Specialist Steve Hammond, is just starting a new career as a teacher. She just went shopping for her fall school clothes and made sure Steve went along. They made a date out of the time together. He enjoys giving his input and has a good eye for colors and patterns that work for Rhonie. He also knew the limit for that month's clothing budget!

Whatever your clothing budget, spend the money wisely. Many people get talked into buying something expensive that really is not that important to them.

Another big trap is sales. Yes, sales. That's because it's easy to see something that is too good a price to pass up, even though it may not look good on us or may not go with anything else in our closet. One of our staff comes dressed very attractively to work each day—even on "casual Fridays." She surprises me when she says a well-tailored and attractive suit came from a consignment shop!

Wear colors that make you feel good. It's amazing how much a color that pleases you will improve your confidence and sense of well-being, and believe me, that will show. If you're serious about wearing the best colors for you, have a color analysis done. Several books and home-based businesses offer this service.[46]

Make sure the clothes you buy are returnable. You know how it is. In the store it seems fine—maybe even better than fine. Yet when you get home it just doesn't look right. Don't finalize the purchase until you are able to see how the item looks and feels in front of your own mirror.

Yes, there certainly are far more important things than how you look, but the fact is, when you look your best you will feel your best, and when you feel your best you are more likely to do your best.

Give Credit where Credit Is Due

All of us, from the most handsome or beautiful to the, well, least attractive, need to practice changing our attitude about our physical appearance. Here are some things to keep firmly in mind:

Every day do one particular thing in terms of nutrition, exercise, and appearance to help you become your physical best. Don't let these things fall to the bottom of your to-do list. Becoming your physical best is a life-long, daily process.

Your physical best means *your* physical best, not someone else's. Accept who you are and give thanks for it.

Look in your daily routine for hidden opportunities to exercise.

Make it a goal to break your bad habits.

Practice looking your best even if you are just with your family. For whom is it more important to look your best?

See yourself as a work in progress, and take pleasure in the changes you see.

> **You can't break a bad habit by throwing it out the window. You've got to walk it slowly down the stairs.**
> **—Mark Twain**

Goals and pointers that move you toward improvement are wonderful, but don't get so buried in them that you neglect to look at what you have accomplished and to celebrate it. Give credit where credit is due. Whenever you pass a mirror, notice something attractive about yourself. Accept that you are you and no one else, and quit making comparisons. In fact, make a commitment to avoid commenting on other people's physical appearance. Stay away from magazines that make you feel depressed with yourself, and focus instead on seeing yourself as God sees you. For the next 21 days, look in the mirror and tell yourself, "I like what I see."

> **The Lord does not look at the things man looks at. Man looks at the outward appearance, but the Lord looks at the heart.**
>
> **—1 Samuel 16:7**

Be in Touch with Yourself

A very good rule for achieving physical balance is these reminders from earlier in this chapter: Listen to your body. When you feel tired, rest. When you are hungry, eat—but wisely—and when you begin to feel full, stop eating. If there is something that constantly pulls you down, take a vacation from it. When you are tempted to doubt the value of the temple God has entrusted to you, reaffirm yourself by reading (or reciting) these words from the Psalms:

> For you created my inmost being;
> you knit me together in my mother's womb.
> I praise you because I am fearfully and wonderfully made;
> your works are wonderful, I know that full well.
> My frame was not hidden from you when I was made in the secret place.
> When I was woven together in the depths of the earth,
> your eyes saw my unformed body.
> All the days ordained for me were written in your book before one of them came to be.[47]

Balance Journal

As you pick up your Balance Journal today, how heavy does it feel in your hands? Heavier than it actually is? We've been talking a lot about the physical side of us, and that may bring up feelings of defeat—especially if exercise or another discipline is something you loathe. We're going to develop some new habits, and as we learned, we have to set aside those "unnatural" feelings and start practicing the habit anyway. The reward for our efforts will show up soon enough. I like to focus on the reward, not the sweat. That's why I celebrate my milestones. I encourage you to do the same as you continue your Balance Journal for this chapter.

Make a new heading called *Physical Balance.*

Write out your thoughts on the following:

- How long has it been since I had a physical exam?

- What types of exercise do I enjoy?

- What foods cause me problems?

- Is God leading me to do a fast? If so, what kind? How long? What is my motivation?

- How much sleep do I get at night? How much do I need? Do I have a sleep debt?

- How might I demonstrate a more balanced approach to my physical life?

Finally, decide on a new habit to form (or an old one to break), and mark out 21 days on your calendar. Force yourself to perform the new habit for those three weeks. At the end of that time, have a celebration. You made it! Then continue the habit, and notice whether it comes more naturally to you.

The next chapter has to do with balance in the mental part of our lives—how to learn for a lifetime, memorizing, goal-setting, and more. You may want to dive right in, or if you need to pace yourself, I suggest you lay this book aside for one to three weeks while you keep focusing on what you've read so far. Do put a date on your calendar, though, that says, *"Read Chap. 4,"* so you won't just give up your efforts toward a well-ordered life. Believe me, our "flesh"—that part of us that wants to live for self and not live dependent on God's grace—will raise its ugly head and tempt you to resist positive change. Instead, cry out to God to help you continue the race, and choose to resist those thoughts of giving up.

.

Chapter 4

Mental Balance

One of the most difficult types of balance for many of us to achieve is mental balance. When we were little, everything was new and there was much to keep our brains active. As we grew older, we were in school. We read, we were constantly exposed to new people, new things, and new ideas. Yet when we reach adulthood and get busy with jobs, families, and all of our many involvements, it is tempting to put our brains on the shelf and take it easy.

What a shame!

Every one of us is constantly changing, and the world around us is constantly changing, too. Aren't those reasons enough to become lifelong learners?

If you still aren't convinced, think about this: Whatever dominates our thoughts long enough will become the dominant passion in our lives.

Wow! We dare not let our minds drift into neutral.

Why should you constantly expose yourself to new things? Because learning leads to learning. Once you get started, you will discover interests you never knew you had. Suddenly you will have something to occupy your mind when you would otherwise be bored and irritated. Instead of standing impatiently in line at the grocery store, for instance, you may find yourself engrossed in reading the labels on your purchases, now that you are more aware of your nutritional needs. Imagine the sense of accomplishment you will get from the new areas of information opened up to you.

Sally and Andrew are a good example. Already in their late sixties, they were sure their years of learning were behind them. Then their grandchildren began talking to them about computers, email, and the Internet. "It was like the children were speaking a foreign language," Sally confessed to me. "We just told them, 'Grandma and Grandpa are too old to learn to use a computer.'"

Then Jesse, their oldest grandson, went off to college on the other side of the country. "We missed him terribly," Andrew recalls. "He was too busy to write and too poor to phone. We called him, but he was always out."

When Jesse came home for Christmas, he told his grandparents, "If you just had email we could really keep in touch. I could let you know about all my classes, tell you what happened during the day, tell you about my friends . . . everything."

Sally and Andrew began to wonder if it just might be possible for them to learn to use the computer, or at least the email function, which the kids told them anyone could do. Some friends gave them a used computer, and their grandchildren went to work giving them lessons.

"That was five years and two computers ago," Andrew says. "Today we are almost experts. We surf the Web, we communicate with missionaries around the world, we have traced our family trees . . . oh, yes, and we 'talk' with each of our grandkids at least once a week. And Jesse is now in Germany!"

Yet there is another benefit to this experience that Sally and Andrew probably don't even realize. They are modeling for their grandchildren the value of learning at any age.

Teach yourself a new language. Become computer literate. Learn to play a new game. Discover a new author. It doesn't matter as much what the subject matter is so long as you are learning.

> **I expect I shall be a student to the end of my days.**
> —Anton Chekhov[48]

Memorizing God's Word, a Forgotten Discipline

I know I just said the act of learning is more important than the subject matter. But let me backpedal a little and say that the *best* way to bring mental balance into your life is to memorize Scripture. Not only will you get the advantage of keeping your brain active and stimulated, you will also have the joy of filling your mind with the revealed Word of God.

You will find that memorized Scripture will bring a surprising strength to your mind and a wonderful perspective to your life. It is one of the best ways to help you determine what your priorities are. And here's a bonus: No matter what your lifestyle, Scripture memorization can be fit into it. Write the portions you choose to commit to memory on 3x5 cards, and use those cards to help you. If you commute to work, use your time at red lights to read over the cards. If you work at home, keep the cards beside you, at your desk, by the phone, or wherever. Keep copies in the bathroom—you can review them while you shave or while you blow-dry your hair. In the kitchen you can review them while you mash the potatoes and stir the soup, and then again while you wash the dishes.

The four "R's" of memorizing Scripture are:

Read

Repeat

Recite

Review

Let's look at each of these separately:

Read the Scripture out loud. What does the passage mean? Why was it written? Read it again, adding an annotation to it that will help you understand the tone in which it was written. Now read it over several times.

Repeat that Scripture again and again, one phrase at a time. This is where the passage really gets embedded into your mind. Repeat it over and over until you can say it by memory.

Recite the Scripture by memory. Don't worry if you stumble. Just refresh your memory, then start again. Practice saying the whole passage out loud from memory until you can do it easily.

Review the Scripture daily. This will make certain that it is permanently etched in you mind. You will be surprised at the unexpected times when the Scripture passages will come back to you.

You might be saying, *"That sounds great, but memorizing Scripture is too hard for me. I can't memorize. I'm just not good at that kind of thing."*

Don't be so sure. There is no such thing as a bad memory, only an underdeveloped memory. Your memory is like a muscle. The more you use it, the stronger and more capable it becomes. So the thing to do is to start using it. Begin to develop your "memory power" and just see how much you can do.

It may be more accurate to say that you don't memorize Scripture simply because there are other things that take higher priority in your life. Again, it's up to you to determine what is really important. Sure, you will be tempted to give up. You will be tempted to spend that commuting time listening to the car radio and your dishwashing time listening to the evening news on TV. But again, it is a matter of priorities. You can choose to get rid of those temptations (turn off the car radio) or to deal with them (close the kitchen door so you are not pulled into the evening news that others are watching in the next room).

One goal of the *read, repeat, recite, review* method of Scripture memorization is to strive for word-perfect memorization. Something that has been extremely helpful to me has been finding a friend with whom I can be accountable, both in my Scripture memorization and in my Christian walk. By learning and reciting together, each of us not only has someone who is counting on us, but we have someone with whom we can discuss the Scripture. In my group of Roosters, we pair off and recite our verses to each other. We have been able to share fresh insights and beautiful illustrations, as well as specific ways in which the Scripture has spoken to us.

Here are some other suggestions to help you in your Scripture memorization:

> **Work on it during a time when your mind is not churning with other things** (not when your boss is making demands, for instance, or when your children are

clamoring for dinner). Many people find that attacking it first thing in the morning works especially well.

Memorize the Scripture reference with the passage. If you don't do this, there will be times when you find yourself struggling to locate just where in the Bible a particular verse can be found.

Write out the verse. Writing helps to get it fixed in your mind. Again, it is nice to have several copies on 3x5 cards that you can post in places where you will see them regularly. Each time you catch a glimpse of a verse card, read the passage.

Say the verses out loud. Speaking the verses audibly does a lot more to encourage memorization than repeating them silently in your mind.

Continue to review earlier verses even as you learn new ones. You don't want to give yourself a chance to forget them.

So where should you begin your memorization? I suggest that you start with Philippians 4:8. In the New International Version it reads this way:

> Finally, brothers, whatever is true,
> whatever is noble,
> whatever is right,
> whatever is pure,
> whatever is lovely,
> whatever is admirable—
> if anything is excellent or praiseworthy—
> think about such things.

I'm sure you can immediately tell why I think it is an excellent one to store in your mind.

Although there are many wonderful verses to commit to memory, please don't limit yourself to learning only isolated verses. Be open to tackling whole sections. They may look a bit intimidating at first glance, but you will find that they will give you a better sense of the flow and impact of the Scripture. Here are some specific sections that I would like to suggest you try:

Psalm 23	Romans 12
Romans 8:35-39	John 15
Micah 6:6-12	Philippians 4

Once you get started, you won't want to stop.

> I know of no other single practice in the Christian life more rewarding, practically speaking, than memorizing Scripture. That's right. No other single discipline is more useful and rewarding than this. No other single exercise pays greater spiritual dividends! Your *prayer life* will be strengthened. . . . Your *attitudes* and *outlook* will begin to change. Your *mind* will become alert and observant. Your *confidence* and *assurance* will be enhanced. Your *faith* will be solidified.
>
> —Charles R. Swindoll
> *Growing Strong in the Seasons of Life*[49]

Learning for a Lifetime

There are so many things I want to learn. There are so many books I want to read, so many people I want to know about, so many places I want to become acquainted with, so many ideas I want to hear about. How about you? Do you want to keep on learning for the rest of your life? I am almost certain you are nodding your head "yes." Very few people actually *want* to become stagnant in life. Yet, unfortunately, many people end up doing just that. Why?

There are ten major barriers to ongoing learning. Let's look at them:

- **Procrastination.** Yep, it's that same old problem rearing its ugly head again. We are constantly besieged by the temptation to put it off until we have more time. That will never happen, and if you wait for it, you will stagnate with the words "someday" on your lips.

- **No follow-through.** You say you have good intentions? Great. But please understand, they are worth nothing if you don't act on them.

- **Lack of preparation.** "Oh, no. I was going to take that class. I didn't realize it was today!" Many people miss out on opportunities to learn because they don't prepare. If there is a deadline, meet it. If there is a date, write it on your calendar. Make learning one of your priorities.

- **Complacency.** Many people are convinced that they already know enough. They do okay the way they are, so why push themselves? That's an unfortunate attitude, because there is so much more available, and you never know what is coming tomorrow. Sally and Andrew were doing all right, too, but if they hadn't learned to use the computer, they would have missed out of so much with their grandchildren.

- **Unrealistic expectations.** "I tried it, but I can't learn it." Really? If this is your excuse, the problem may well be that you made the mistake of assuming you could pick up a new skill immediately. None of us can. We do not learn as easily as we once did, and we don't learn as quickly as our children do. Yet that doesn't mean we can't learn. It just means we need to cut ourselves some slack. Each of us learns and progresses at a different rate.

- **Quitting too soon.** Discouragement always seems to be lurking around the corner. We get frustrated when we see someone else learning faster than we are. Someone makes some crack about our work. We think we are doing well and then we seem to hit a blank wall. Yes, all these things happen. Yet if learning is a high priority, you will pick yourself up and move forward.

- **Accepting failures.** Failure is a strange thing. It can drive us into the ground with despair or it can be our best teacher. You will have failure; how you handle it is up to you.

- **Avoiding risks.** One big temptation for many people is to play it safe. That way, they figure, there won't be mistakes to pull them down. Certainly it doesn't make sense to behave recklessly, but playing it too safe is boring and gives you no chance to grow.

- **Saving energy.** Another big temptation is to automatically assume your energy will be better spent somewhere else. Don't allow yourself to get caught in a trap! In other words, stay within the things you "should" be doing and learning and don't waste your resources on frivolous things. Discover the adventure and joy of learning something just for the fun of it.

- **Letting other people discourage you.** "I've always wanted to learn Spanish," a woman I know said. I asked her if she was going to do it and she said, with a sigh, "No. I mentioned it to my family and they all laughed." Don't allow unsupportive people to cause you to give up. What you learn and when you learn it is your personal choice. All that really matters is what *you* think is important. Once you make that decision, say *adios,* go off to class, and do it.

Whether you think you can or you think you can't, you're right.

—Henry Ford

The Secret of Growing Better

"I want to go back to school, but I'm 45 years old," a man said. "If it takes me four years, I will be 49 by the time I graduate!"

Guess what? In four years that man will be 49 whether he goes back to school or not! We all will be older tomorrow than we are today. Next week we will be even older, and next year older still. This is true whether we are 25 or 45 or 75. Life doesn't stand still. Every one of us is constantly growing and changing. It's the changes we make today that will make the difference in whether we are older and wiser tomorrow, or just plain older.

At CLI, *growth* is one of our core values. Years ago, we started what we call "Summit University" to assist us in this growth process. We all reach high in our learning (like a mountain climber pursuing a summit) by reading at least one book a month and discussing it with the rest of the staff. We all do it, from the youngest to the oldest person on our staff.

I am determined to age well and not get "just plain older." Are you, too? Good for you!

A really good place to start is to stretch yourself by taking an educational risk. There are a number of ways you can do this. You might . . .

- take a class outside the scope of your present interests and expertise

- work toward a degree (with the help and encouragement of family and friends, I finished my doctorate since the original edition of this book)

- start and lead a book club

- take an art appreciation class

- take an astronomy class

- learn to play an instrument

- learn a new computer program

- take an introductory foreign language class

Get the idea? With a little thought, you will be able to fill in more ideas of your own. With a little more thought, you will be able to choose an exciting challenge for yourself. Once you get started learning new things, you will find that there is an increase in your skills and confidence, and that will lead you on to still more learning.

A Minute Found

"But I just don't have time!"

No time. This is the most common argument for not accepting a new challenge. It's not a totally unfounded one. Yet all of us—yes, even you—can find some time, if not in hours then at least in minutes. Believe it or not, a minute is enough to sharpen your mind and learn something new. Robin Harshbarger, CLI's Chief Program Officer, jokes about building a machine that will give us more time in the day. She may still be working on her invention, but in reality, she has figured out that the secret is balancing her priorities, it isn't a matter of creating more time. We can always find a few extra minutes in the day to do the things we really care about.

> **We cannot do everything at once, but we can do something at once.**
>
> **—Calvin Coolidge**

Make it a rule always to carry something to read along with you. Keep a supply of crossword or Sudoku puzzles you can take on airplane trips or to appointments when you know you may have to wait. When you commute, listen to recorded sermons or books. Do you carpool? Listening to these materials can lead to great discussions! Bring your weekly magazines or newspapers along to the gym or to the doctor's office. Not only will you sharpen your mind, but you will find that waiting is much less frustrating if you have something to do.

Sharpening your mental powers doesn't have to be work. There are lots of fun brain-trainers. Try some of these:

- working crossword puzzles

- playing board games that introduce you to new facts and trivia

- playing checkers, chess, or other strategy games

- playing word games that build your vocabulary

- making up stories for children

- engaging in games that make you think on your feet, like charades

- renting how-to videos that teach you to build something or do something new

- renting travel videos, or videos about different countries or cultures

May I make a suggestion? If you decide you want to be a person who learns for a lifetime, begin to create a *learning atmosphere* around you. Here are some ways to do this:

Designate a favorite spot for reading, such as a comfortable chair near the window, where the light is good. Keep a good book or a couple of magazines nearby—maybe even under the chair.

Set up a writing corner with a journal, a couple of pens, and paper for writing notes. How about landscaping your back yard or patio as an *outdoor* getaway for journaling?

Keep 3x5 note cards, a pen, and a Bible in a particular place. As verses or passages of Scripture you would like to commit to memory come to mind, jot them down and put them in the same place. Periodically fill out the cards and have them ready for your next Scripture memory session.

Create a learning idea file. Clip interesting articles, book reviews, or other things on which you might want to follow up. Be sure to review your file periodically.

Read the newspaper or watch the news. Try a world news program on TV or online that expands your knowledge beyond your local issues.

The good thing about learning is that you can practice it at any time and any place it will fill those small chunks of time you spend waiting in lines, laying over in airports, riding in the car, or sitting in the doctor's waiting room. It can fit right into your everyday situation, whatever it may be. You will find classrooms in the strangest of places, and teachers among the most unlikely of people.

Learn from everyone.

—Ben Franklin

Setting Goals

Accidental learning is wonderful and a great use of spare time. Yet the most productive learning of all will occur when you make up your mind to do something, set a goal, then pursue that goal and accomplish it. Again, people are different. I have a way that works for me, but it might not work so well for you. Some people find planning and goal-setting helpful and encouraging. Others would rather live day to day without a lot of thought for the future. Which type of person are you? If you're not sure, look at these statements. Check the box by the one that most sounds like you:

- ❐ I carefully plan everything I do.

- ❐ I sometimes plan, but not always.

- ❐ I make plans for specific activities, like having a party or going on a trip, but I certainly don't chart the course of my life.

- ❐ I don't plan much of anything unless it's absolutely necessary.

If you checked the first one, you are an *avid* planner. If you checked the second, you're an *organized* planner. If you checked the third, you're an *under-stress* planner. If you checked the last one, you are an *organizational avoider*.

There are advantages to planning, but there are pitfalls as well. First, let's look at the *avid* planner. What happens to you when you plan a dinner in advance, down to the smallest detail, only to have a storm come up that makes you have to cancel everything? Also, if you plan everything, where have you left room for healthy spontaneity?

The pitfalls for the *organizational avoider* are more obvious. Think about the poor man who makes a call the night before the big party to the young woman he expected to take—only to find out she's going with someone who asked her two weeks before. An *organizational avoider* has spontaneity down pat, but often suffers the consequences of not planning.

Are you somewhere in between? An *organized* or *under-stress* planner? What might some of your pitfalls be?

Everyone has to set some goals, no matter what type of planner or avoider they are. You can plan more or you can plan less, but you cannot avoid goal-setting completely. Goals are a necessity, not a luxury. Do you want to be successful? I cannot think of a single successful person who did not start with a clear definition of goals.

Goal-setting is not just an exercise for, say, business executives. Establishing your goals is really putting your hopes and dreams on paper in a measurable way. Do you have a sense of calling in your life? Don't procrastinate. Set your goals around that mission and put tangible dates to those goals. Most importantly, write them down.

Even when it comes to goal-setting, however, balance is the name of the game. Many people make the mistake of trying to achieve a dream by sacrificing all the other areas of their life. A man I'll call Matt knows that from personal experience. When he was eight and his sisters were five and two, his father decided to quit his job as a struggling pastor and get a medical degree. He did accomplish that goal, but it took a horrible toll on the family. For eight years, they lived on a shoestring budget. Matt's mother cleaned houses and took in laundry in an effort to keep meat on the table. When Matt started high school, he rebelled against everything his parents had stood for. His mother, exhausted and discouraged, left the family. The girls went to live with two different relatives. Matt stayed with his father, but since Dad was never home, Matt was completely unsupervised.

He got into all kinds of trouble, finally getting arrested for car theft.

Was Matt's father's goal worth it? Maybe or maybe not. Was the unbalanced way he went after it worth it? When this question was posed to Matt's father, tears filled his eyes. "I lost my family," he said. "What do *you* think?"

Healthy goal-setting goes beyond focusing on just one aspect of your life. It means deciding what you want your entire life to look like. And it takes into consideration how your decisions will affect others. It means seeing your life in balance.

Should you have goals? Absolutely! Not only is it wise, but it is a divine assignment. Look at these words of Paul:

> Therefore we do not lose heart. Though outwardly we are wasting away, yet inwardly we are being renewed day by day. For our light and momentary troubles are achieving for us an eternal glory that far outweighs them all. So we fix our eyes not on what is seen, but on what is unseen. For what is seen is temporary, but what is unseen is eternal.[50]

When Paul says we fix our eyes on the eternal, I look at that as us having our priorities in place, our goals set. Notice how those other things that are temporary and troubling just fade out of the picture? Paul knew the secret of setting his mind on the things above, and everything else just fell into place. That is goal-setting at its best.

Balance Journal

There are so many exciting things to learn about—and so many mental exercises we can do to brush the "cobwebs" out of our brains! Try these stimulating activities as you continue your journal with the heading *Mental Balance:*

Get up and look out the window. Study something outside for one minute. Look away and describe it in detail.

Write down the names of all fifty states—or as many as you can in two minutes.

Pick an age between 5 and 20. Try to remember where you lived at that age, who your friends were, what pets you had, and so forth.

What are all the things you learned in the last 30 days? (Write those down and you'll surprise yourself how much you learned.)

As you consider the prospect of learning for a lifetime, here are some questions to ask yourself:

What is the best book I've ever read? Why did I like it so much? Are there other books like that that I would like to read?

What is one subject I've always wanted to study?

What is one skill I'd like to learn or improve?

Chapter 5

Emotional Balance

Your neighbors stop by for coffee and a long chat. Your son badgers you to let him drive the car across town to his friend's house at night time. Your coworkers want you to join their softball team. Your brother and sister-in-law want you to join a book discussion group.

Which of these activities will contribute to your emotional balance?

All of them, if you really want to say "yes"; none of them, if you really want to say "no." Saying "yes" when you want and need to say "no" is a major energy-drainer, and one of the most common causes of emotional imbalance.

So why do we do it? Why do we say "yes" when we really want to say "no"? Most often it's because of fear, or because of a false sense of obligation. At any rate, it is most unfortunate. Not only is our time wasted, but as we are doing that thing we really don't want to do, resentment builds up in us. That resentment chews away at our energy and self-esteem and destroys our emotional balance.

Often, people lace their requests with flattery ("You are so good at working with people! I just love the way you can talk to anyone. Oh, if only I had that gift."). Or they use that old standby: guilt ("You're the only one who can do this. Without you, the whole program will be a flop"). With flattery, it feels good to be indispensable. With guilt, it feels downright awful to look like the bad guy if you don't cooperate.

These are such powerful techniques of manipulation. But the fact is, if you can't do what they're asking of you, they will find someone else. Every day indispensable people get sick, move away, and say "no," and the world hasn't stopped turning yet. No one is really concerned about your priorities except you, and you will feel a greater sense of accomplishment and self-worth by spending your time on those priorities. Remember, it isn't a question of which is good and which is bad. It's a question of which is better than good, and which is best of all.

"That's the problem!" you may be saying. *"I can't decide which is best, and I'm so worried that I'll make the wrong decision."*

Okay, let's tackle this thing called anxiety next—it certainly contributes to imbalance in our emotional lives.

Indecision, Worry, and Anxiety

Indecision and worry and anxiety are negative mental habits that serve no useful purpose. Paul wrote, "Do not be anxious about anything, but in everything by prayer and petition, with thanksgiving, present your requests to God."[51]

Yep, that's what he said—don't be anxious. Just don't do it! No, it wasn't easy for him. Don't forget, he wrote most of his letters from prison. That would cause anxiety in the best of us.

Yet the fact is, worry and indecision exact a huge toll on us. When we are worried or anxious, we don't exhibit that well-ordered life we desire. Furthermore, those emotions don't accomplish one thing. No problem is ever solved by worry. No decision is ever made by worrying about it.

Sure, you will have decisions to make; sometimes extremely important ones. But instead of allowing yourself to worry, I suggest that you imagine your various options and mentally "try each one on." How does each look on you? How does it feel? Choose the one that is right and gives you the most peace of mind. Once your choice has been made, stick to it. Refuse to allow yourself to wonder about any of the other options.

Suppose it isn't a decision that is causing you emotional imbalance. Suppose it is just general worry or anxiety that is haunting you. Here is a suggestion: Take out your Balance Journal and write down everything that is troubling you. Look at each item you wrote down and ask yourself, "Is there anything I can do about this specific concern?" If the answer is "yes," promise yourself to take constructive action. If the answer is "no," let go of it. Cross it out of your journal and symbolically cross it out of your life.

One of the best ways to beat anxiety is to look back at God's faithfulness to you in the past. If He has always met your needs before, can't you trust Him to meet them now?

So, identify the negative emotional habits in your life:

- disorganization
- not knowing your priorities
- a pattern of worrying
- an inability to make firm decisions

Then work and pray toward eliminating them. Refuse to let them waste your valuable time or sap your energy any longer.

When you are able to turn the worry and anxiety over to God and let Him take it from you, "the peace of God, which transcends all understanding, will guard your hearts and your minds in Christ Jesus."[52]

> **The discipline of emotions is the training of responses.**
> —Elisabeth Elliot
> *Discipline, the Glad Surrender*[53]

Emotional Rest

We have talked about the importance of physical rest. Without it, our bodies cannot continue to function. Yet what about emotional rest? Just as physical rest gives our bodies a break from physical activity, emotional rest gives our minds respite from the wear and tear of anxiety, fear, tension, irritation, depression, unhappiness, and emotional fatigue.

What is emotional rest? It is peace, quiet, tranquility, contentment, and emotional refreshment. It involves allowing our minds to rest from intellectual pursuits so that our emotions can also relax.

Notice the overlap of the emotional and the spiritual when it comes to rest. We already talked about spiritual balance through rest—especially Sabbath rest. Consider these emotional restoratives below. They will also greatly affect our spiritual balance:

> **Pause in your busy life to help others.** Volunteer your time at a soup kitchen, a hospital, or a shelter for the homeless; or deliver food to shut-ins via Meals on Wheels. It will help you to take your eyes off yourself and to see through the perspective of someone who has greater needs than you do.

In your Balance Journal, keep a calendar of your emotions for a month or two. This will help you to see what pulls you down and what brings you up.

Make an ongoing list of things you're grateful for. Don't forget the things most of us tend to take for granted—sight, a brain that works, a home in a free country, the freedom to worship God.

Make a list of things that make you happy. Keep it handy and add to it as other things come to mind.

Refuse to feel sorry for yourself. Don't let negative circumstances control you. Read books, watch videos, and listen to messages about people who have overcome the most severe circumstances. You might want to start with Corrie ten Boom's autobiography, *The Hiding Place*. She spent years in a Nazi concentration camp where she watched her sister die—but she spent the rest of her life testifying to God's goodness and mercy, and the transforming power of forgiving one's enemies. Or consider Joni Eareckson Tada, who at the age of 17 broke her neck in a diving accident. Although destined to spend the rest of life as a quadriplegic, she has inspired millions all over the world through her art, music, writings, and speaking.

Find a special place that refreshes and inspires you. It might be a park bench, a mountain trail, a stretch of beach, a path in the woods, or even a corner of your own backyard. Use it as a regular retreat in which to read or reflect.

Schedule a quiet time every day to meet with the Lord and pray. Make this a priority and say "no" to anything that would interrupt you during that time.

Let everyone know that unless there is a true emergency, no one is to disturb you during your quiet time.

Seek out friends who build you up and bring out the best in you. No, I don't mean friends who flatter you or say only what you want to hear. I mean those who encourage and inspire you to be the best you can be. I meet regularly with a couple of friends at a local coffee shop or we go exercising together. They encourage me to continue developing my strengths and inspire me to reach for new heights. I do the same for each of them. When we are done with our meetings, we feel renewed and ready to take on the challenges the world brings our way.

Take a vacation from something. Take a vacation from TV, for instance, or from answering the phone (let it go to voicemail). In the interest of emotional balance, how about taking a vacation from complaining or criticizing?

Close your eyes and picture your greatest achievement. Is it owning your own home? Having a successful marriage after experiencing your parents' disastrous relationship? Building a good business? Parenting great kids? Introducing someone to the Lord? Savor those achievements and let them give you the emotional refreshment you need.

Emotional Balance through Solitude

Leadership guru John Maxwell has his "thinking chair." E. Stanley Jones had his "listening post." I have the high desert terrain near Phoenix, Arizona. These are our places of welcome solitude. I absolutely crave solitude! We talked about this in the chapter on Spiritual Balance, but it warrants repeating here because of the benefit to our emotional lives.

What might be a place of silence and solitude for you? Perhaps you don't crave it like I do, but decide anyway on a specific place that will be your special place. Pick a specific time when you will go there to spend time with the Lord. Be encouraged by this biblical promise: "If any of you lacks wisdom, he should ask of God, who gives generously to all without finding fault, and it will be given to him."[54] You don't have to be clever and plan everything out during your times of solitude. Just listen to the Spirit of God and to His Word. Let Him work on those deep-seated emotions that have been churning in you. Let Him affirm who you really are to Him, and He will bring you into the emotional balance that you crave.

Be still, and know that I am God.

—Psalm 46:10

Express Gratitude

Every day, make it a practice to find something for which to be thankful. Gratitude costs nothing and pays off so handsomely. The summer of 2000 was a difficult one for me. My organization, Celebrate Life International, was still very young. Summertime tends to be a tight time financially for nonprofits. That summer was no exception for us. We had to lay off staff— and it was extremely hard to find a sense of joy and balance in the midst of all the pressure. Then, out of the blue, I got a telephone call.

"Zig Ziglar is on the line for you," my assistant told me. I looked at her and said, "Yeah, right." "No, he really is!" she said. "At least that's what the guy says. He told me he's Zig Ziglar."

I figured that one of my friends was playing a joke on me, because many knew that Zig Ziglar was one of my role models. He is so good at demonstrating how to have a positive perspective, and how to live life according to your priorities.

But this was not a good day for a joke. Still, the light was flashing on my phone, so I thought, *Well, I'll just give whoever it is a piece of my mind.*

"Well, hello, Zig Ziglar!" I said a little too enthusiastically. "How are you?" And from the other end of the line came a voice, saying, "Hey, Lori. How are you?" As soon as I heard his greeting, I knew it really was he, because I've listened to so many of his tapes.

"Zig Ziglar!" I said. "I can't believe this is really you!"

"Lori," he said, "I want you to know that the other day, I heard from a common friend of ours about what you're trying to do in this country, how you're trying to impact the educational system of the United States of America with biblical truth and with principles. And I got to thinking that has to be heavy for you sometimes. So I decided to call you just to encourage you. Lori, you have a great vision and a great calling. No matter how difficult it becomes, always remember that if you can find the things you're thankful for, and if you can be grateful for all you have, and you can focus on that rather than on what you don't have, then that will get you through the heaviest times."

"Zig," I said, "I know that you and I have never met, but you have been such an encouragement to me."

"Well, you know what encouragement is?" he asked. "It's putting courage into somebody's life. And one of the best ways that you can do that is to help them see the positive. Help them be grateful for the things they have, and then say to them, 'You can do this!'"

I was so encouraged after that phone call! How important it was to have someone remind me to be thankful for the things I have instead of focusing on what I don't have.

In the summer of 2000, just when things at CLI could not have gotten any worse, I received a renewed spirit. I had a renewed confidence to approach significant contributors (we call them "investors" because they are literally investing in the lives of young people) to give sacrificially. Money started coming in again, and we were able to rehire the staff. Gratitude on our part prepared our organization to see God's provision released in His perfect timing.

A good way to remind yourself to be grateful is to keep a memory book or a list of things you can look to as your own Altars of Gratitude. (Your Balance Journal, of course, is a great place to start recording these.) When you look back at your Altars of Gratitude and remember how God provided for you in those circumstances, it will renew your faith that He can and will meet your needs today.

A few months ago, we brought Shawn Naidu on staff as our Country Administrator for CLI in Cape Town, South Africa. When we welcomed him on board, I was reminded and thankful all over again for the encouragement I had received several years before to keep persevering. Had I not kept going, I would have missed out on the great privilege and blessing to make a difference in the lives of young people in the country of South Africa.

There was another thing I got from that experience with Zig Ziglar. I realized that when God brings somebody to my mind, I need to be faithful to follow through with that person. Zig will never know how much fresh air that telephone call breathed into my weary soul. Breathing in the fresh air is very important. To achieve the balance, however, you need to breathe it out again. Receive and be revived, then give out again. A very important way to practice gratitude and to encourage one another is to help each other see the things for which we can be thankful. Take some time to identify the things in your day that are God's way of reminding you that He is faithful and that He is in control. At the top of my list that day would have been that short phone call.

Develop Your Strengths, Not your Weaknesses

Have you noticed how emotionally draining it is when you're forced to work within your weaknesses? Here's an example that may fit your situation: You own your own business and need a website. If you're like me, and don't know the first thing about web design, you'd be extremely frustrated to try to design your own site. Instead of taking a class on how to build your own Internet presence (a class I know I wouldn't enjoy), wouldn't you be better off hiring someone to do that for you?

I strongly believe in spending the majority of our time developing to the max those areas in which we are already strong. Some of my strengths include being a visionary and communicator, and working well with people. I am not a detail person, however, and doing clerical work does not come easily to me. I know that I have to learn how to balance my time, and I do so with my PDA ("Personal Digital Assistant"). It helps me make sure that I can keep my appointments, that I show up at the right places at the right times, and that I know what I am supposed to be doing. I have not, however, attempted to become my own administrative assistant. Instead, I have surrounded myself with people who have the gift of organization and who are detail-oriented. Instead of putting a great deal of time and effort into working on that weakness, I maximize on what I have by working within my strengths.

Not sure how much to focus on your weaknesses? Ask yourself whether your strong areas are being undermined because of a weakness. If so, then devote just enough time on that weakness to get your strengths back into full swing. An example for me was to ask Jodi Willard, my very able assistant, to train me in the use of my PDA. I didn't need to know how to program the thing, just use it for appointments and contacts. Then I could be more effective in what I do best: communicating with all those people in my PDA who needed my attention.

Make the most of what God has given you. I challenge you to run in the freedom of what you're good at by further developing your strengths. You see, it is not a good return on your investment when you try to fix your weaknesses. No matter how much time you spend on them, you will probably stay weak in those areas. We simply need to spend just enough time on our weaknesses to keep them in check. Our best course lies in letting others shine in those areas where we are weakest, while we, in turn, concentrate on those abilities with which we have been blessed. We all need to work within our strengths.

Never Give Up

How can we have balance emotionally if we give up too easily on the things that clearly fit within our priorities? In my senior year at Seattle Pacific University, I had to take a sociology class with all the freshmen. I have to tell you, I had an attitude when

I entered that classroom. I mumbled, "Oh, brother! I can't believe I have to take this class with a lot of freshmen." It just seemed so beneath me.

We took our first test and I found it a little bit challenging, but I didn't think much of it. The next week when we came to class, the instructor had put the test scores up on the board, starting with the highest score and going on to the lowest. "Oh, man," I thought, "I really feel sorry for that person who got the lowest grade. Some dumb freshman who thought school was nothing but youth camp. Well, he'll learn."

You guessed it—that lowest grade was mine. I was so humiliated!

"Hey, Lori!" my friends were calling. "What did you get on your test?"

"Oh," I said, "I'd rather not say."

One of the girls said, "She probably got the highest grade in the class and doesn't want to brag."

A guy across the room said, "No, she didn't. I got the highest grade!"

Oh, great! I thought.

"So what *did* you get?" the guy asked.

"Well, I just don't want to say," I repeated, trying my best to sound humble and not as humiliated as I felt.

When Kurt came to pick me up that night, I was fit to be tied. "Kurt, I got the lowest grade in that whole class of freshmen. Can you believe this school? They obviously don't realize how lucky they are to have me as a student, or they wouldn't treat me this way. I mean, they gave me the lowest grade in the class! You know what, Kurt? I'm going to quit! I'm not going to take this kind of treatment! I'll do great things and validate my ministry, and I don't need them to do it!" I went on, and on, and on, and on, but the gist of all I said was, "I quit! I quit! I quit!"

I finally stopped, and we just walked in silence for a while. After a few minutes Kurt said, "So, I'm married to a quitter, am I?"

Wow! That didn't feel very good.

He shook his head and said, "I'm married to a quitter and I'm going to spend the rest of my life with a woman who couldn't handle a bad grade."

That did it. "If you think I'm going to quit over a small grade, you have another think coming!" I announced. "I'm not going to quit! I don't care how many bad grades I get, I'm not going to quit!" On Monday morning I went back to that class with a completely different attitude.

Do not give up! Don't do it! Whether it's a grade or something far more devastating, like a marriage hanging in the balance, the Lord Jesus Christ would say to your heart, "I've given you My Spirit, and I will enable you to run the race. I will help you go the distance." Hang in there. No matter how bad it gets, you must not give up. I am not asking you to become a doormat and endure a tough situation; I am encouraging you not to give up while you take action and follow a plan that will result in turning the situation around for the best.

You know what I want on my tombstone? *We couldn't keep her down.* I will never, ever give up on the important things of life.

How about you?

Simplify Your Life

A wonderful way to move toward emotional balance is to get the clutter out of your life. Many of my friends have a junk drawer (some of them even have a junk closet!) Every now and then it happens that they are frantically looking for something in there, but so much stuff has collected that they can't find anything. So, desperate and frustrated, they start throwing out all the unnecessary stuff, hoping that they'll be able to find what they really care about.

Well, that just may be what you need to do with your life. You may need to take inventory and say, *"What is all this stuff? Why am I filling up my time with junk and crowding out all the good stuff?"* As you begin to sort, ask, *"What can I eliminate so that I can get some order and balance in my life?"*

That's what it means to simplify your life—simply to get rid of those things that are taking you away from emotional balance at its best. Wherever you are going, you do not need to drag along any emotional baggage. As I get older, I have worked hard to do this consistently. Kurt and I have been happily married for 26 years, yet we are not able to have children. It was sad to me to realize I would never hold my own baby in my arms. I had to learn to channel those feelings of sadness and depression into something positive. I chose to concentrate on unique ways I could serve as a visionary leader to reach millions of young people with truths that transform. Today I can honestly tell you that although I see motherhood as a wonderful thing, I no longer have those feelings flood over me. I have eliminated that emotional baggage from my life.

> I think people are so preoccupied with material difficulties. In the industrial world where people are supposed to have so much, I find that many people, while dressed up, are really, really poor.
>
> —Mother Teresa
> *Words to Love By*[55]

Emotional Buffers

Where can you find your own personal islands of emotional comfort? What is it that energizes and restores you? What is it that gives you . . .

more energy?

a calmer day?

a better attitude?

the desire to go on and on?

the determination never to give up?

Here are the answers some people gave to that question:

Tracy: "Warm water. I love to swim for energy and take a bubble bath to relax."

Suzanne: "Going outside. Whether it's cycling, walking, or just sitting at the beach contemplating, being outside is both energizing and calming."

Rich: "If I'm active, biking. If I'm quiet, crossword puzzles."

Tom & Lara: "Pick-up basketball. We play it whenever we can. Then in the evenings, when we need to relax, we watch old musicals on TV."

Walt: "Gardening. There is nothing as restorative as getting down in the dirt and making something grow."

You say not one of these appeals to you? No problem. Simply find what does. When you find what energizes you, what restores you, and what relaxes you, you are well on your way to achieving emotional balance.

I like this A-to-Z guide to emotional balance:

Accept yourself as you are.

Believe in yourself.

Consider the lilies.

Don't sweat the small stuff.

Envision the whole of you—even the unfinished parts.

Find humor in life.

Give unconditionally.

Help someone anonymously.

Influence a child for the good.

Join in on something fun.

Keep close to God.

Laugh out loud.

Meditate on a psalm.

Never give up on yourself.

Offer your gifts for the good of others.

Play restorative music.

Quit worrying.

Read books that encourage you.

Savor God's Word.

Think before you speak.

Understand the value of solitude.

Value yourself.

Whisper a prayer in the morning.

eXamine your priorities.

Yell when you need to.

Zap back to reality when you must.

Winston Churchill was invited back to the boys' school he had been kicked out of when he was a child. Now that he was famous, he had been invited to speak in an assembly before the whole school. He stepped up to the podium, waved his fist in the air, and said, "Never, never, never, never, never, never, never, never, never give up." And then he sat down.

That's it! When you get struck down, you get back up. When you are knocked low, you get back up. When you're crushed, you pull yourself together and get back up. When you feel like you are being persecuted on every side, you endure the pain and get back up.

You may be hard pressed on every side, but you will not be crushed. You may be perplexed, but you will not yield to despair. You cannot despair when you've got the Lord living in you. You can be persecuted, but you will not be abandoned. You can be struck down, but you will not be destroyed.

My favorite chapter in the book of Romans assures us, "We are more than conquerors through Him who loved us. For I am convinced that neither death nor life, neither angels nor demons, neither the present nor the future, nor any powers, neither height nor depth, nor anything else in all creation, will be able to separate us from the love of God that is in Christ Jesus our Lord."[56]

Wow!

Talk about emotional balance.

And it's all yours.

Balance Journal

Write down the words *Emotional Balance* and then explore these questions:

> What am I feeling right now?
>
> What emotions cause anxiety in me? What will I do about those emotions?
>
> What could help me achieve more balance emotionally?

In the interest of emotional balance, you must:

> **Work on your attitude.** Start a list of the things you're thankful for. You can make a habit of it by adding to it whenever something comes to your mind. Why not dedicate some pages of your Balance Journal to be your "Altars of Gratitude"?
>
> **Schedule fun time for yourself.** What could you drop and just do right now? And what could you plan using goal-setting that would be satisfying to you down the road?

For immediate encouragement:

List three things you've most enjoyed . . .

. . . in the past week.

. . . in the past month.

. . . in the past year.

. . . in your life.

Chapter 6

Balance in Relationships

Remember your first grade report card? It told your parents whether you were good or bad, smart or disappointing, promising or pathetic. It probably reported whether you tended to talk too much or too little, whether you played nicely or needed to learn to share, and whether you followed directions or did your own thing.

Before the first report card, most of us had no idea that the opinions of virtual strangers could affect and influence our parents' approval of us. In fact, those report cards may well have been the beginning of that difficult balance of relationships with which we all now have to deal. From those very earliest experiences some of us grew to believe that the most important relationship skill was to learn to please people. What an unfortunate lesson, for people-pleasing is neither godly nor healthy.

The goal of people-pleasing—or appeasing—is to make sure that people like us. Yet what actually happens is that those who do the pleasing or appeasing usually end up feeling used, unappreciated, and driven to become all things to all people in order to maintain their image. It becomes a vicious cycle to continue to seek approval. At first appearance, people-pleasers seem thoughtful and giving, but in fact they are slaves to the insatiable need to be admired, needed, and loved.

This results in relationships dangerously out of balance. There can be no well-ordered life when people-pleasing defines us and our relationships.

Family Relationships

In Chapter 1, I had you list your current priorities and then distinguish between your "should" priorities and your true priorities. Go back to that section where you honed your list down to your three top, true priorities. Were they goal-driven, such as "Becoming a proficient reader" or "Having children before we're in our 40's"? Or principle-driven such as "I must quit telling 'little white lies' even when it is convenient to do so"?

Let's look now at another list of priorities. I like to call it the "Divine Order." These don't "trump" your other priorities. They may, however, influence you in such a way that you'll feel you need to adjust some of your goal-driven and principle-driven priorities.

Look at God's creation. There was an order to it. We will do well to prioritize our relationships the way God prioritized creation:

- God comes first—that's obvious
- Marriage comes next, then
- Children
- Work
- Ministry

I often see couples put their marriage very low on the list. It's not necessarily a question of how many hours you spend at each of these relationships, but of how *interruptible* the time is with each of those priorities. Think about the pastor who is sitting at dinner with the family. The phone rings or a parishioner comes to the door. Does this become an interruption or does it become an opportunity for that pastor to keep family a priority? Healthy boundaries may dictate that the pastor reschedule a visit with the parishioner or ask the caller to call back at a later time. Sounds simple, doesn't it? But too often we let interruptions rule us. It's a tell-tale sign that our priorities are not lining up with the Divine Order.

Fortunately, when we seek balance in our relationships, we discover that there is a lot of overlap. Time with the whole family, for instance, keeps the two following priorities in tact at the same time: Marriage and Children. Do you have a regular prayer time? Great. But it's not enough! "Pray without ceasing," Paul exhorts us.[57] How do we do that? Try praying under your breath when you're at work. Or be aware of God's presence with you when you spend time on a special date. I was certainly praying during that school assembly when I had to speak to such a rude student body. Interesting, isn't it, how the human mind can speak, pray, and freak out at the same time? When we give our other priorities over to God in this way, we are keeping Him in first place in the Divine Order.

> The Christian home is the Master's workshop where the processes of character molding are silently, lovingly, faithfully, and successfully carried on.
> —Richard Monckton Milnes

Let's look more closely at putting (or restoring) balance in these relationships—starting with marriage and the home. If you are single or without children, feel free to skip the parts that don't apply to you, although I trust we can learn from all the sections in this chapter. You never know when you might have an opportunity to share an insight into the lives of a married couple or a family that has children—even if this is not your own experience.[58]

Begin by establishing a home that is warm, hospitable, comfortable, and a haven of rest and peace to all who live there. All day long you, your spouse, and your children are with people who criticize, tear down, cause anxiety and stress. Life just has a way of beating everyone up. For that reason, make your home just the opposite. Let it be a haven of peace, encouragement, love, and joy.

"That sounds great," I can almost hear you saying. *"But you obviously don't know anything about my family life."*

No, but if your family is like most today, you don't have much time. Perhaps both you and your spouse work, or maybe you are a single parent who holds down two jobs just to make ends meet. Perhaps you live with your parents because you can't afford your own place, so you are scrimping and saving every dollar you can earn. Or maybe for the same reason, you are living with roommates, or are sharing a house with another family.

Whatever your situation, you are not alone. Juggling family, work, and living situations is a concern in most. Remember what we've been learning about prioritizing. Find those most important things that truly need to occupy your time and attention. Building a welcoming home environment could be one of those. The other, less important tasks will balance themselves out—or maybe they just need to be eliminated, guilt-free, from your schedule. Just establish your priorities according to the Divine Order.

Couples Together . . . Or Not

When families feel squeezed for time, very often it is the relationship between husband and wife that suffers the most. They know the importance of spending time together, but there just isn't any time for sharing romantic moments. They say:

"When our schedule is freer . . ."

"When the kids are older . . ."

"When I catch up at work . . ."

"When our grown kids get places of their own . . ."

". . . then there will be time for us."

Yet that time comes so infrequently—if it ever comes—that many couples simply drift apart. By putting off shared romance, the two soon find that warmth and passion have disappeared from their relationship.

The sad fact is that many couples give their pets more time and attention than they do their own relationship. We'd never expect Felix or Fido to thrive without food and water, a good word, and a scratch behind the ears. Yet somehow we expect our marriages to grow and flourish without any time or attention.

"But what can I do?" you may be crying out in desperation. *"I'm not just saying I'm too busy. I really am too busy!"*

Good news! Romance doesn't have to be time-consuming. Look at the following suggestions and see how many you can put into practice with your own spouse. However, don't try these just once or twice. You may feel sort of awkward at first. Keep it up for a month or so and see if there isn't a warming trend between you.

Celebrate you daily homecomings. What do you do for the first five minutes you are both home? Look at the mail? Listen to the answering machine? Mediate fights among the kids? Take the dog for a walk?

Change that pattern. You see, the first five minutes you are together is crucial, because it sets the tone for the rest of your evening. Leave the mail and the answering machine, send the kids to their rooms for just five minutes or have them walk the dog. Then focus exclusively on each other. Sit together on the sofa and tell each other about your day. Hug and kiss. Give each other a neck rub. Hold each other and just sit quietly. It's only five minutes, but those five minutes will remind you that you are a team working together toward a great goal—the success of your family.

Help your spouse help you. One of the most destructive of emotions is resentment, the very one many spouses—especially wives—feel when it seems their partner isn't doing his or her share of the work. A 1993 Families and Work Institute study found that men think they are doing more housework than their wives think they are: 43 percent of dual-income husbands said they were doing half the housework, while only 19 percent of dual-income wives felt that way. Interesting, isn't it? Yet to any individual, perception is reality. If you feel that your spouse isn't holding up his or her end, talk to him or her. Share your frustrations constructively rather than allow them to build up and wear on your relationship. Together, make a list of the things each should be responsible for around the house and make an agreement that each will take care of his or her own responsibilities. Then let your spouse take responsibility. Don't jump in to pick up the slack.

Surprise one another. Small surprises do a lot to put energy back into a relationship. Notes with expressions of love, relevant Scripture verses, or just an appropriate message ("I'll be praying for your sales meeting at 10:30") mean so much. Small gifts or flowers at unexpected times, cards that express a special sentiment, or even bringing home Chinese food on a busy day show you care.

Practice random acts of thoughtfulness. Put out his vitamins in the morning. Record her favorite TV show. Pick up a magazine that features an article that will be of special interest to your spouse. Cut an appropriate and interesting article out of the paper. One couple I know is especially good at this. He makes her a cup of hot cocoa from scratch every morning, and she takes the comics out of the newspaper and puts them in the bathroom for him! Those little actions might not mean much to anyone else, but they demonstrate love to the two of them.

Transform ordinary moments. It's just an ordinary night after the kids are in bed and the dinner dishes are washed. Yet why not make it extraordinary by snuggling up in front of the television, holding hands like you used to, and toasting each other with a glass of sparkling cider? Or how about giving each other backrubs? Or lighting a fire in the fireplace and reading to each other in the warm glow? It's just an ordinary night, but it can be transformed into something so special.

Plan date nights. Most married couples have long since stopped dating. Big mistake! Once a week or once a month—whatever you can arrange—plan to get away together. And once you've set your date, don't break it except for the most serious of reasons.

"I know all those things," you may be saying. *"I haven't done them yet, but I intend to start . . . sometime."*

Good intentions are a beginning, but they don't go far enough. Focus on what you *actually* do rather than on what you *want* to do or what you know you *should* do. Do you come up short? Then do something about it now, before it's too late.

Relationships with Your Children

You have probably heard about the studies that show how little time families actually spend talking with one another. A 1994 Angus Reid poll, for instance, found that television watching was the main activity parents did with their children (an average of 6.3 hours per week). Other activities, such as reading to one another or helping with homework, received a mere 2.1 hours per week.[59]

Of course, TV allows you to just sit placidly and not do anything, an idea that sounds very appealing when you are tired after a long day at work. If you just wait for family interaction to happen, it may not—or at least not the way you want it to. Once again, you need to be proactive and *make it happen*. Here are some suggestions:

Go with routines. You say your children don't like routine? Let me assure you, they will adapt. In fact, you will likely find that they even appreciate it. It gives them security by helping them know what to expect. If they know Saturday is laundry day, Sunday is church and then family day, Monday is grocery-shopping day, and so on, they won't be nearly so likely to badger and whine and complain about what they want to do. Discuss the routine with everyone, make the decision, then stick to it. By teaching your children how to schedule their day—get up at a certain time, feed the dog before school, do homework before dinner, watch one video or TV show, go to bed at a set time—you will be teaching them a valuable life-long skill.

Assign and post family jobs. When family members know exactly what is expected of them, there are not nearly so many arguments and misunderstandings, and there is much more peace in the family. Write down each person's job assignments along with spaces to check off when the job is done. Post the list where everyone will see it (the refrigerator seems to be a favorite place). Then reward those who have all of their jobs checked off for an entire week (ice cream, popcorn, and extra time before bed are always popular rewards).

Don't expect perfection. Not everything is going to go according to your definition of perfect. Sometimes someone will drop the proverbial spinning plate. Accept and deal with it. If you don't, you will continue to fight a losing battle and everyone—especially you—will be worn to an emotional frazzle. Does it really matter if Jimmy's bed isn't made perfectly? Or if the laundry isn't folded exactly as you would do it? Your spouse may have a different way of mashing potatoes or making the bed, but does that really matter? Your children may not be that great at doing the vacuuming or dusting. So what? You will live longer—and a lot more happily—if you adopt a policy of "it's good enough" on those things that don't matter as much. Save your high standards of excellence for the things that really matter, such as your children's character development.

Consider outside help. It's very difficult for some of us to get it through our heads, but some things are worth paying someone else to do. It just may be that the hourly wage you would pay someone to clean your house—or at least to do the heavy cleaning—would really be worth it when compared to how the time and stress take their toll on you. Or what about the yard work or the dripping faucet in the bathroom? If you enjoy working with your hands—and have the time— go for it! Turn it into an opportunity to apprentice your eager child as a gardener or plumber. But if it's something you dread, think about hiring the boy next door or paying a handy friend to fix the drip for you. Don't only consider the cost; also consider the emotional benefit of having someone do it for you.

Streamline your own schedule. Instead of going grocery shopping on your way home from work every evening, save yourself a great deal of time and trouble by making a list and going shopping only once a week. If you can manage it, shopping at times and on days when there are fewer people in the stores will help you avoid long checkout lines. When you run errands, group them together by area so you don't end up driving back and forth across town for something you forgot. Streamlining takes only a small amount of organization and planning, but the time and family stress you can save are considerable.

Set aside family time. As with any relationship, it's important to plan time for your family to be together. Make time for regular family days—such as Sundays—when everybody is usually available. This doesn't have to be an entire day. Just a few hours would be great. You might go to church together, then have a picnic or play a game your teens would enjoy, like disc golf, or fly kites or swing on swings with your younger children. What you do isn't as important as the fact that you are spending the time together doing something enjoyable.

Trust your own decisions. What if your boss asks you to work on Sunday? Or you put in overtime on the night of your child's piano recital? What if he or she insists that you spend a good deal of your time on the road? It's scary to say "no" to your boss, yet you resent having this intrusion into your family time. What do you do? Certainly I would never suggest that you take your job lightly. Yet if your priority is your family, you may need to speak up. Talk with your boss about your concerns. You may be happily surprised to find that he or she is pleased to work with you to discover a solution you both can accept. If not, you might want to start looking for another job, with a company that is more family-friendly.

Praise the efforts of others. Everyone needs a pat on the back and a word of appreciation. When someone in the family does a job well, or does something extra just to help out, or makes any extra effort, be quick to praise and generous with your hugs and kisses. A smile or a thank-you encourages everyone to keep up the good work.

Reward yourselves. Becoming a united family with healthy relationships can be tough work. When you see positive steps, even baby steps, congratulate each other and treat yourselves. Take the family out for ice cream. Go to a movie together. Take in a sporting event you all enjoy.

Don't allow outside interruptions. The phone rings while Junior is telling you about what happened at school today? Let it ring. Unexpected visitors stop by while you are helping your daughter with her science project? Tell them it's nice to see them but that you are busy at the moment. Don't be ashamed to let people know that your family time is a high priority to you.

Grab serendipitous moments. That unplanned time you just happen upon can be the best relationship-building time of all. When your son is shooting baskets and says, "Hey, Dad, how about some one-on-one?" When you have just crawled in bed and your daughter peeks in and says, "Mom? Can I talk to you?" When you have fifteen minutes to spare before you have to leave for work, just enough time to whip up some hot cocoa for you all to share. When your kids call out, "Look what's on TV!" and you pop a bowl of popcorn and sit down to watch with them. When the casserole is in the oven and the table is set, and you can sit on the floor and build Lego's with the kids for a few minutes. Don't let those minutes slip away. They are precious!

Divert, Withdraw, Abandon

Balance in relationships, as in other areas of our lives, requires rest and relaxation. Without it, we cannot go the distance. I really like Rick Warren's formula for lasting. He says:

- Divert daily

- Withdraw weekly

- Abandon annually

What does this mean, practically speaking? Well, to **divert daily** means to take a little "vacation" every day. This could be getting a large mocha at a favorite coffee shop, watching highlights from football games, enjoying a hot bath with candles burning and music playing, or grabbing a twenty-minute nap in the middle of the afternoon.

To **withdraw weekly** means to take at least one day off each week. You might partner with other parents and take their kids for a day, then allow them to reciprocate by taking yours. It may mean going for a long bicycle trip, or if you are married, packing some snacks and taking your spouse on the trip. Depending on what you enjoy, this could be anything from a game of golf, to a day of shopping, to breakfast with friends, to a visit to the art museum.

To **abandon annually** means to take a yearly vacation. It may mean traveling somewhere, or it may mean going camping close by, or it may mean staying home but not answering the phone or the door. In almost every community there are things to do and see and enjoy that residents never get around to pursuing.

Divert daily, withdraw weekly, abandon annually. It really makes a lot of sense, doesn't it? If you are rested and refreshed, getting your relationships in balance will be much easier.

Friendships in Balance

We all need friends, even the most private of us. We need one another's encouragement, mentoring, and love. We need to be accountable to one another. And we need to know we matter to people outside our own family.

"Snowflakes are fragile," the saying goes, "but if enough of them stick together they will stop traffic." It's true for snowflakes, and it's true for people. If you have friends who will stick with you through thick and thin, you can withstand the disappointments, difficulties, and unfairness of life.

We need to have friends, and we need to be friends.

> **God evidently does not intend us all to be rich, or powerful or great, but He does intend us all to be friends.**
>
> **—Ralph Waldo Emerson**

Positive versus Negative

I can't choose who is going to come my way in need of my help, but I can choose who I hang out with. Part of finding balance in our lives is finding out which relationships are truly beneficial and which merely clutter up our lives. It sounds harsh, but it is reality. Are there some relationships in your life that simply need to go?

We have to watch out for "Beleaguered Buddies." These are the "friends" who never get around to committing to their own goals. Instead, they pull you into their procrastination with them. They stop by your home or office to complain about their nasty bosses or their awful spouses or the churches they won't go to because they are full of hypocrites. If anyone suggests that they just might be able to improve their lives, their attitude becomes one of helplessness: "You just don't know how hard I've tried!" or "Nothing ever works out for me. If anything can possibly go wrong, it will!" or "No one will ever give me a break."

Beleaguered Buddies are extremely high-maintenance people. They will cause you to waste many valuable hours of your time, and they will sap you of emotional strength. Life is too short to be constantly pulled down. Instead, seek out friends who inspire you and encourage you to be the best you can be.

> **The perfect friendship is that between good men alike in their virtue.**
>
> **—Aristotle**

Instead of listening to the water-cooler gossip that pervades your work environment, take your coffee break elsewhere. Is the lunchroom a breeding ground for complaining by your coworkers? Instead of being dragged down by their conversation, use your lunch period to go for a walk or run some errands. Put on earphones and listen to music.

You have the right to say "no" to maintaining friendships with people who rob you of your balance. Negative people are balance-robbers. You will do well to avoid them. I'm not saying that you shouldn't take the opportunity to speak truth and friendly correction into negative people's lives. I'm saying we need to choose who we invest time with for our friendships. If we develop relationships with negative people, we will be dragged down with them.

I have personally had to confront friends who were not being positive about their life and their circumstances. In one case, the friend *was* willing to change and we enjoyed a much better friendship as a result of that. In another case, the friend felt insulted by my request and did not see a need to change at all. Sadly, I had to put space between us because I could not afford to be around that kind of negativity. Nor can you. The world already has plenty of negative people—we need to concentrate on the positive whenever we can.

What about people who seem like good people—everybody says so—but you are leery of building a friendship with them? Well, everybody may be right in noticing that the person is a good person. They may even be a good friend for someone else—just not for you. Don't give in to peer pressure. Yes, *listen* to others, but *trust* yourself. Choose your friends wisely. Relational balance requires that you nurture those relationships that bring peace, harmony, and balance into your life.

> **Friendship is unnecessary, like philosophy, like art....** **It has no survival value; rather it is one of those things that gives value to survival.**
>
> —C.S. Lewis
> *The Four Loves*[60]

Flowers for the Living

Sometimes I'll be out with some girlfriends—maybe hiking in the clean outside air, or maybe lunching at a favorite hole in the wall—and I'll stop everyone and say, "You know what? This is a sacred moment. Right now, right here, we are having a sacred moment together."

If we can learn to recognize these moments, we will be able to look back later and cherish them all over again, and again, and again. I was in Venezuela with a group of twelve or thirteen people. We were climbing way up in the Andes Mountains. We looked out on the beauty of the mountain range, the clouds below us, and all the greenery. It was so beautiful that it silenced us all. None of us could say a word because of the breathtaking beauty. After a few moments of silence, one by one, many of us began to weep. Still, not a word was spoken. There was no church music, no sermon, no religiosity. There was nothing but the sound of God's creation, yet it spoke to us in such a profound way that the tears rolled down our faces. Then one of the guys in the group, Chris, who has a fantastic voice, began signing a hymn while we all looked at the magnificent view. We all joined in.

After those moments of silence, weeping, and singing, we looked at one another and realized that we had experienced a pristine time of worship. Still, no one dared to talk. Finally, one girl, a new believer, looked at me and whispered, "Lori, what is this? What's happening here?"

"It's a sacred moment," I said. "It's a holy moment. It's a moment where we worship simply because we are aware of God's presence. He visited us in a moment that we don't ever want to forget. We want to be able to return to this moment again and again."

The power of memories can bring us a great deal of balance. When we are in the midst of a hectic moment or a discouraging circumstance, when we are ill or sad, when our friends have let us down and everything seems wrong, we can go back to that moment and regain our balance. I can go back to Venezuela, back to the Andes Mountains, back to that moment when nothing was spoken; only gentle singing was heard and tears were shed. I can go back in my memory to the time when God visited us.

Where have you experienced sacred moments, and with whom? It is important to recognize them.

Yet it is difficult to have sacred moments if we allow things and people to crowd out all the sacred spaces in our lives. Sacred moments, when God's Spirit visits us and brings well-being to our souls, happen when we create sacred space in our lives. So protect that sacred space. Refuse to allow anything or anyone to crowd it out.

I am so big on sacred moments that some of my friends tease me and say, "Lori, is this a sacred moment?"

I don't mind. It's important to me to verbally remind people to acknowledge these times in our lives.

Just as our sacred moments will pass unnoticed if we aren't attuned to them, so will the goodness and love of friends pass unnoticed if we fail to acknowledge it. If we are going to achieve relational balance, it is vital that we slow down the pace of our lives and pause to give people the flowers due them while they are still around to enjoy the fragrance.

My mom used to tell us kids, "You know, people always wait to give folks their flowers after they are dead. They bring them to the funeral and lay them before the casket. But the people can't smell them then. They can't see and enjoy them after they are gone."

This doesn't mean you need to actually hand each person a bouquet, of course. No, the way to give people flowers while they are living is to come up with something positive about each person's character or personality and then give that person his or her "flowers" by speaking a thoughtful word, sending a note, or making a phone call. It doesn't have to cost a thing, yet it can mean so much.

To whom would you like to give a special "flower"? Why not set aside time today to make a call or write a note?

Relational Rest

When you have your relationships in balance, you will experience a special thing called relational rest. This simply means that you will have a sense of peace and harmony with other people. Just imagine! Peace and harmony in your home, in your church, in your school, in your workplace—indeed, throughout your community.

Relationships of peace and harmony don't come about unless you have a heart of love and a soul that is at peace with God. As a matter of fact, your spiritual, physical, mental, and emotional rest are all deepened and brought into balance when you receive the gifts of the Spirit offered through Christ Jesus.

> But the fruit of the Spirit is love, joy, peace, patience, kindness, goodness, faithfulness, gentleness and self-control. Against such things there is no law. . . . Since we live by the Spirit, let us keep in step with the Spirit.
>
> —Galatians 5:22-23, 25

We all need fellowship, and we need deep friendships—ones that are steeped in prayer, free for vulnerable sharing, and filled with forgiveness. We all need friends who encourage balance in our lives.

Balance Journal

In the section *Balance in Your Relationships*, copy your three true priorities from the first chapter in the book. Now that you know more about the Divine Order, do you need to replace or revise any of those goal-driven priorities? If so, go ahead and write them down.

Now take a look at your family relationships. How are you encouraging balance in your family?

> Your family may include your spouse, your children, your parents, your siblings, your parents-in-law, your roommates, or whoever else has a regular family interaction with you.

How would you describe the balance in your other relationships? With your friends, coworkers, neighbors, those you share a hobby with, your church acquaintances?

Look at the fruits of the Spirit listed in Galatians 5:22-23.

> Which ones do you see flourishing in your life?

Which ones do you need to nurture?

Are there special people who encourage the fruits to flourish in your life? How might you give "flowers" to those people while they are still living?

Chapter 7

Celebrating Balance at Its Best

In going through this book with me, and keeping up with your Balance Journal, I trust you have done a great deal to bring balance to your life in these pivotal areas:

- spiritual

- physical

- mental

- emotional

- relational

Good work! Now you have one more thing to do: **Celebrate!**

I recently had to take my car to the shop. They told me it would take two days to get it fixed. I felt inconvenienced by the whole process. Why couldn't they get it done faster? They said it had something to do with ordering a part. I made a couple of phone calls and José Maldonado, our company's Chief Operating Officer, volunteered to pick me up and take me to the office. He showed up in his jacked-up 4-wheel-drive Jeep, with all-terrain tires, no roof, and no doors. Kurt and I love Jeeps, so getting picked up in one was a highlight for me that day. I jumped in and we drove to the office. With my hair flopping in the wind I started screaming, "Yahoo!" It felt as if I was on vacation. People driving by us looked at me and wondered what I was so happy about in my office clothes. If only more of us would go to work each day with the same spirit as when we leave on vacation. What a better and balanced life we would enjoy!

Certainly you should celebrate your accomplishments, goals, and decisions, but don't stop there. If your life is to be truly balanced, put on the crowning touch by determining that celebration will be a regular part of your life. Celebrate frequently and celebrate well. Good and frequent celebrations will bring a sense of joy to your life.

You say you do celebrate? You say Christmas and Thanksgiving are big times for you? That you never miss a birthday or a graduation? That you even make a big deal out of anniversaries and Valentine's Day?

That's great. However, I'm not simply talking about the big times in your life. I'm talking *frequency*. Even when there isn't a big reason. Even when there isn't time for a real bash or money for nonessentials. Actively watch for small reasons to celebrate, and when you find them, snatch them up. You'll discover that they will bring a renewed joy to your existence and will contribute balance to that emerging well-ordered life of yours.

When I was a student at Fuller Theological Seminary, I worked long, hard hours. One year, during finals week, the workload was especially heavy. My classmates and I were learning Hebrew and Greek, and we had theology classes that were especially difficult. One of the girls we hung out with was from England. I remember walking out of class one day, every one of us burdened down with books to read and homework to do. There just weren't enough hours in the day and night to do it all. We didn't even have enough energy to complain, so we just walked along together in silence.

Suddenly the girl from England announced, "Tomorrow afternoon at two o'clock I want you all to come to my house."

I looked at her as if she was out of her mind. "What are you talking about?" I exclaimed. "I don't have time to come to your house!"

"I don't have time, either," each of the other girls chimed in.

"All I'm asking for is three-quarters of an hour," our British friend said. "I want you all to meet at my house for just 45 minutes' time. That's all."

Although not one of us felt we had 45 minutes to give, we all grudgingly agreed to meet her. It was, after all, less than an hour, and we did want to be kind to her. So we all showed up at the appointed hour, and there, in her front yard, in the glorious Pasadena, California, sunshine, she had a lovely table all set up. It was just a picnic table, but it was covered with a pretty tablecloth and there were candles and flowers in the center. On the table were teacups and a matching teapot, and there was a plate of delicious-looking scones. Right there, in the middle of a hectic finals week, we had an honest-to-goodness English tea party.

For 45 minutes, all of us girls sat around that little picnic table. What a relief it was to set aside our worries and labors and share such fun and laughter. What a gift to have that small, unexpected island of diversion in the middle of such a hectic schedule.

In England, our friend told us, they considered it most important to take time out of the day and drink tea. Yet when the 45 minutes were over, she said a prompt good-bye, and we all left, renewed, restored, and truly thankful.

When I look back on my seminary education, that impromptu tea party is one of the moments I will never forget. That day, sitting in the sunshine around that lovely picnic table, I learned the importance of celebration. To this day, in my marriage, in my relationships, at work, in every area of my life, I make it a point to stop at unlikely moments and celebrate. I want to do it frequently and I want to do it well.

> [Moments of seeing beauty] are the pinnacles of our experience, lifting us out of the dreary circumstances and giving us pleasure and delight until we fall back and again become our ordinary selves. They must be interwoven into our daily existence in order to make life endurable and sweet. If we do not train ourselves to receive beauty when it appears before us, our memory bank will be filled with only the products of the mind, the will, the intellect—cold, logical, and calculating—without serenity, heart, humor, or warmth.
>
> —Luci Swindoll
> *You Bring the Confetti, God Brings the Joy*[61]

One thing that makes it possible to celebrate frequently and spontaneously is to have things already in place, just waiting for an occasion to celebrate. One thing I do is buy nonalcoholic sparkling cider whenever I find it on sale. I try to always have a bottle of it waiting in my refrigerator. Because I so love impromptu celebrations I want to be ready for them. If someone comes home with an "A," if good news comes in the mail, if something goes well at work—even if there is a very simple reason, such as the garden doing well—we can pop open a bottle and celebrate.

What are some things you might have ready for a celebration? It all depends, I know. So it's best to have things on hand to allow you to celebrate events with the various people who may be in your life: a spouse, children, your friends, your coworkers, your visiting guests. At CLI, we keep our refrigerator stocked with sodas and water. That way, even when the delivery guys drop off a package, we can have a quick one-minute celebration with them. They love it when they have to deliver to our office!

Your celebration items might differ from mine, but here are some suggestions to keep on hand:

- candles
- colored paper streamers
- confetti
- balloons
- party stickers
- brightly colored napkins
- ice cream and cones
- a favorite frozen dessert
- a frozen pizza
- bottled bubbles for blowing
- handmade coupons for favorite treat spots such as an ice cream shop, a movie theater, the garden center, a video rental store

I know one family whose "spontaneous celebration" collection fills an entire hallway cabinet and contains a selection of small, inexpensive gifts such as note cards, stickers, and small treats. "We buy things after the season, when they are half price," the wife explained. "A small valentine stuffed animal, for instance, can say 'I love you' any time of the year. Jelly beans after Easter are always a treat. A mug specifically aimed for 'Daddy' or 'My Dear Sister' can be just the right thing. Anyway, who says we can't have a little bit of Christmas in the middle of July?"

Celebrate Your Gifts

God calls us to do great things, and best of all, He gives us the ability to do them. When we seek His will, and desire above all else to follow His plan and His commandments, then our ambitions and goals are pleasing to Him. When we are pleasing Him, He takes pleasure in our celebration. Do you doubt this? Consider this assortment of verses from all over the Bible:

> Then all the people went away to eat and drink, to send portions of food and to celebrate with great joy, because they now understood the words that had been made known to them.[62]

> They will celebrate your abundant goodness and joyfully sing of your righteousness.[63]

> You will sing as on the night you celebrate a holy festival; your hearts will rejoice as when people go up with flutes to the mountains of the Lord, to the Rock of Israel.[64]

> "My son," the father said, "you are always with me, and everything I have is yours. But we had to celebrate and be glad, because this brother of yours was dead and is alive again; he was lost and is found."[65]

Remember what God has done!

Remember where you are headed!

Remember who you are!

You were created to celebrate!

Yesterday, Today, Someday

Yesterday you likely celebrated less than you now wish you had. Today you are trying to make celebration a greater part of your life. Someday...ah, someday. Someday you will do the wonderful things of your dreams. Someday you will see the pyramids of Egypt. Someday you will write the story of your family. Someday you will visit Rome, Cape Town, and Sydney. Someday you will run a marathon race. Someday you will bike across your state. Someday...

Do you know what your "somedays" are? They are your dreams and goals. Of course, some are more dreams and others are more goals. What about *your* somedays? Are they dreams or goals? Here is an easy way to figure it out. Ask yourself, "If money were no object, and I had no obligation to anyone, would I jump out of bed tomorrow morning and be on my way to do that 'someday'?" If you would, it is likely a true goal. If you would crawl back in bed, however, and say, "Maybe some other time," then it is probably just a distant dream.

Someday Folder

If a someday is a dream, go ahead and enjoy dreaming, but realize that's all it is. But if your dream is a goal, begin now to bring it to reality. Start by making it as tangible as possible. A good way to do this is to put together a "someday folder." Collect things that will demonstrate your someday goals. For instance, if your goal is to build a sailboat, begin to collect building plans. If your goal is to make your backyard into an English garden, start gathering pictures of English gardens that appeal to you. If your goal is to make a handmade quilt, begin to collect quilt blocks and pictures of quilts that strike your fancy.

A someday folder is more than just a collection of wishes and whimsies. It is a hands-on plan for what will very possibly be real one day.

> Far away in the sunshine are my highest aspirations.
> I may not reach them,
> but I can look up and see their beauty,
> believe in them,
> and try to follow where they lead.
>
> —Louisa May Alcott

One of my somedays that I have already accomplished was to go to India to see Mother Teresa's work in action. (In fact, I have been there five times so far.) The sisters there seem to have such a sense of peace and well-being in the midst of incredible circumstances and a schedule that is unbelievably challenging. The first time I was in Calcutta, one of the most impressive things to me was the sisters' prayer time. They pray before they do anything. For them, prayer is truly a key thing. It meant so much to me because prayer is such a key part of my life, too.

To be perfectly honest, though, it also almost irritated me. The sisters had such an incredible ability to stay centered. They actually seemed to be at peace right down to their inner core. So I went up to one of the sisters and asked, "How do you all get this way?" I mean, we were standing in the middle of unbelievable poverty and sickness and disease and death. People were literally dying on the doorsteps. They had hundreds of kids there, as well as hundreds of leprosy patients. There were sick and homeless people everywhere. And yet, in the midst of it all, these sisters had an almost palpable sense of peace.

"How do you do it?" I asked, looking around me. "How in the world do you do all this?"

That humble woman looked at me, smiled, and said, "Lori, Lori. You're worried and bothered about so many things. It's really very simple. We pray and we obey. It's moment-by-moment surrender."

"I know that," I said a bit impatiently. "But what I mean is, *how* do you achieve that peaceful disposition?"

"Lori," she said, "if you did what I just said, you would not be asking me this question. It is moment-by-moment surrender. It is praying and letting God bring the idea to your mind. Then it is doing what God tells you to do."

I came away from the experience finally realizing the truth of what that sister had told me. It truly is moment-by-moment. That peace really is a matter of surrendering each and every moment in whatever we do. Are you feeding your baby or changing a diaper? Are you meeting an impossible deadline at work? Are you commuting in rush-hour traffic? Are you enduring an unbelievably difficult person? Are you mowing the lawn, or doing the laundry, or picking up toys off the floor? These can be moments of worship for you. Because for a child of God, everything you do—*every single thing*—is to be done as unto God. That is the way these sisters brought such a wonderful sense of balance to their existence. That is what led to such great peace under the most un-peaceful of circumstances.

Even in the immediate, hectic aspects of life, we can have that moment-by-moment surrender to the Lord. We can pray to Him anywhere and under any circumstance. We can surrender whatever He brings into our minds. That obedience will bring about order to the depth of our hearts, and that well-ordered heart will lead us to joyful celebration.

I learned all this because I had a tangible someday in mind and took the steps necessary actually to visit Mother Teresa's work in India. I encourage you to build that someday folder. You will be surprised to discover what great experiences await you.

> **Lord Christ**
> **Your Servant**
> **Martin Luther**
> **said he only had**
> **two days**
> **on his calendar:**
> **today**
> **and "that day."**
> **And that's**
> **what I want too.**
> **And I want**
> **to live**
> **today**
> **for**
> *that day.*
>
> —Joseph Bayly[66]

Growing Older Joyfully

I talked earlier about us staying sharp mentally as we get older. We need to learn for a lifetime and never "retire" our minds. But there is a lot of propaganda in our society that can discourage older adults. Our culture puts a great deal of emphasis on youth. *Look young,* we are told. *Act young. If you allow yourself to grow old, you are no longer of value.* I beg to differ. Growing older is a natural part of life. Ideally, growing older also means growing in wisdom and maturity. Shouldn't that make it something to be desired?

When we are young and inexperienced, we look for role models and mentors. For a season in my life, one of my personal mentors was writer-speaker Luci Swindoll. She has been especially important in my life, because she has been a special kind of mentor—a joy mentor. Here is what she has to say about growing older:

> Growing older can be unbelievably exciting. It can truly be a joyful experience as we look for new paths of broadening our minds, enlarging our horizons, loving different people and new things, reaching across prejudicial barriers. Simply put, it takes getting outside ourselves and creating what is not, balanced and blended with getting inside ourselves and accepting what is.[67]

All my life, I have been involved in a special "prayer and share" time with my family. Kurt and I have carried on this tradition in our own marriage. As we grow older, it has become an even more precious part of my life. "Prayer and share" takes place at the end of the day. Each person gives one prayer request and one highlight of the day. It gives us a chance to reflect on the ways in which the Lord has worked in each of our lives during the day.

This is a great thing to do as a family, but it is also something you can do alone. Before you go to bed, ask yourself:

What has God done *for* me today?

What has He done *through* me today?

What does He want me to surrender to Him tonight?

God got your attention through something today, didn't He? He spoke to you through particular events of your life, right? He showed you once again the importance of communing with Him. Once again He drew you into praise of Him. God was truly at work. This kind of reflection will give a whole new meaning to your life, day after day. Every day we get older, but every day is another opportunity to celebrate life and celebrate God. This is celebration at its best.

Wow!

Be joyful!

Celebrate!

On the Threshold of Tomorrow

Although you rejoice and celebrate today, tomorrow will be even better. You have learned new things and you have been introduced to new experiences. Tomorrow you will encounter . . .

- increased opportunities
- increased experiences
- increased service
- increased wisdom
- increased satisfaction
- increased peace
- increased joy
- increased celebration

How you react to today is the key to what you will experience tomorrow. You don't know what is coming in your future.

None of us does. Yet what actually happens is not what will determine who and what we will be. Two people can experience exactly the same circumstances. One will be devastated while the other is encouraged and strengthened.

> **Two men looked through prison bars; one saw the mud, the other saw the stars.**

Look past your problem, and you will see God's purpose. Guess what? God's purpose is always greater than the problem. That's the truth that will enable you to go the distance.

> We have the idea that God is leading us toward a particular end or a desired goal, but He is not. The question of whether or not we arrive at a particular goal is of little importance, and reaching it becomes merely an episode along the way. What we see as only the process of reaching a particular end, God sees as the goal itself. . . . His purpose is for me to depend on Him and on His power *now*. If I can stay calm, faithful, and unconfused while in the middle of the turmoil of life, the goal of the purpose of God is being accomplished in me. . . . His purpose is the process itself. . . . It is the process, not the outcome, that is glorifying to God.
>
> —Oswald Chambers
> *My Utmost for His Highest*[68]

Dear friend, you are on your mark!

Get set!

Go!

Run the race, and run it to the finish line. Your greatest celebration of all is still to come. It will occur on that blessed day when the Lord says to you, "My good and faithful servant, I am pleased with your race."

Balance Journal

Wow, let's party! In this final section of your journal called *"Celebrate!"* create your Someday Folder. Start your list of "somedays":

Which ones are merely distant wishes?

Which ones are possible future realities?

Begin your own "prayer and share" time. List the significant things that have happened to you today.

How did God try to get your attention?

What did you learn from this?

Reflect upon the meaning of your day.

For what can you praise God today?

Plan a simple celebration—and then party on!

I have had an ulterior motive in having you create your Balance Journal. I wanted you to experience the forming of a new habit. What is your "style" of journaling? Do you just write short phrases that reflect the "bottom line"? Do you write reams as you regurgitate your thoughts onto paper? Could you make this into a fun exercise? Did a new habit form in you over the time you took to read this book and fill in the journal? I purposely didn't include space in this book itself for you to fill in the blanks. I wanted you to create a separate journal so you can continue this habit long after you've passed this book on to a friend. Gordon and Gail MacDonald now have a treasure trove of journals that fill several bookshelves. They can look back on those works and rediscover God's faithfulness to them over the 40 years they've been doing it. My prayer is that you will establish balance in all areas of your life, and that your Balance Journals will be a cherished roadmap of the journey.

As you continue on life's journey, keep seeking balance. Not partial balance. Not mediocre balance. But go for balance in all areas, 100 percent. Balance at its best!

Endnotes

1 J.B. Phillips, *Your God is Too Small* (New York: Macmillan, 1961) 56.

2 "Nielsen Media Research Reports Television's Popularity Is Still Growing," 2007, The Nielsen Company, 24 Aug. 2007 <http://www.nielsenmedia.com/nc/portal/site/Public/>.

3 2 Corinthians 3:17-18.

4 "Maxwell Maltz: Psycho-Cybernetics Expert," 2007, Self-Growth.com, 16 Aug. 2007 <http://www.selfgrowth.com/experts/maxwell_maltz.html>.

5 See Philippians 4:8.

6 Psalm 84:10 (NASB).

7 Psalm 91:1-2.

8 M. Robert Mulholland, Jr. *Invitation to a Journey: A road map for spiritual formation* (Downers Grove, Ill.: InterVarsity, 1993). This text is an interpretation of Psalm 131:2.

9 Frank Barker with Maureen Rank, "The Martha Syndrome," 2007, The Navigators, 7 Aug. 2007 <http://www.navpress.com/EPubs/DisplayArticle/1/1.44.8.html>.

10 Mother Teresa, *Words to Love by* (Notre Dame, Ind.: Ave Maria Press, 1983) 44.

11 *The Confessions: Saint Augustine* (Works of Saint Augustine, a Translation for the 21st Century: Part 1 – Books) (Hyde Park, N.Y.: New City Press, 1997) 39.

[12] Siang-Yang Tan, *Rest: Experiencing God's peace in a restless world* (Ann Arbor, Mich.: Vine Books, 2000).

[13] Philippians 4:6-7.

[14] Gordon MacDonald, *Ordering Your Private World* (Nashville: Oliver-Nelson, 1985) 128-129.

[15] 2 Corinthians 5:18.

[16] 1 Peter 3:15.

[17] Lawrence J. Crabb, *The Safest Place on Earth: Where people connect and are forever changed* (Nashville: Word, 1999).

[18] *Wild Women of God* is a registered service mark of Celebrate Life International, Inc. and is licensed exclusively to Designed for Excellence, Inc. Find out more about *Wild Women of God* conferences and other seminars at www.DesignedForExcellence.com.

[19] Tony Stoltzfus, *Leadership Coaching: The Disciplines, Skills, and Heart of a Coach* (Charleston, S.C.: Booksurge, 2005) 7-8.

[20] *Leadership Coaching* 8.

[21] *Leadership Coaching* 15.

[22] Rebecca Langer, e-mail correspondence, 8 Aug. 2007. Rev. Langer is a member of the Presbytery of St. Augustine, Jacksonville, Florida. She worked closely with the program of Christian Spirituality at San Francisco Theological Seminary.

[23] James Emery White, *Serious Times: A life that matters in an urgent day* (Downers Grove, Ill.: InterVarsity, 2004) 89.

[24] My meetings with Gail MacDonald last about 36 hours and are intense. We follow up with phone calls and emails in between these meetings. But I also considered Mother Teresa a spiritual director for me in the 1990's. I met with her on four separate

occasions, and had about four minutes with her each time. Sixteen minutes compared to 36 hours with Gail—very different, but both were significant experiences in spiritual directing.

[25] In the next chapter, you'll learn about my nonprofit organization, Celebrate Life International, and the *Teach One to Lead One°* program for mentoring youth. Is there a *Teach One to Lead One°* work near you? Make a difference by becoming a mentor!

[26] *Words to Love by* 79.

[27] Maxwell Maltz, *Psycho-Cybernetics* (New York: Pocket Books, 1960), vi.

[28] *Psycho-Cybernetics* xiii-xiv.

[29] Celebrate Life International was founded in 1996. *Teach One to Lead One* and *Celebrate Life International* are registered service marks of Celebrate Life International, Inc. Find out more about CLI's exciting programs for youth—especially at-risk youth—by visiting www.CelebrateLife.org.

[30] *Psycho-Cybernetics* xiv.

[31] Some suggest drinking one ounce of water for every two pounds of your weight. In other words, if you weigh 150 lbs., drink 75 oz. of water a day.

[32] Richard J. Foster, *Celebration of Discipline: The Path to Spiritual Growth* (New York: HarperCollins, 1978).

[33] *Celebration of Discipline* 3.

[34] Elmer L. Towns, *The Beginner's Guide to Fasting* (Ventura, Calif.: Regal Books, 2001).

[35] Elmer L. Towns, *Knowing God through Fasting* (Shippensburg, Pa.: Destiny Image, 2002).

[36] During the first day, you'd eat breakfast and lunch, then start your fast by skipping supper. The next day you skip breakfast and lunch and end your fast by eating supper.

[37] *Celebration of Discipline* 3.

[38] I find Bill Bright's advice on fasting to be very helpful: http://www.billbright.com/howtofast/. Also check out Ron Lagerquist's extensive site at http://www.freedomyou.com/.

[39] Jesus' admonition to keep fasting between you and God had to do with combating pride. Fasting isn't always to be "secret" but usually we're to be "quiet" about it. Sharing your experience with someone close to you can keep you accountable and guard you from the physical challenges that sometimes accompany fasting.

[40] One leader of a faith-based organization fasted 40 days each year for several years. Obviously he lost a lot of weight during those times. But he would gain it all back—and more—after the fast was over. This is unhealthy. It takes its toll on the human body to deprive and then indulge in food.

[41] "How Much Sleep Do We Really Need?" 2007, National Sleep Foundation, 23 Aug. 2007 <http://www.sleepfoundation.org/>. The online article points out further that each individual is different in their sleep needs, but the numbers given here are a "rule of thumb."

[42] "Sleep Is the New Status Symbol for Successful Entrepreneurs," 2007, *The Wall Street Journal*, 23 Aug. 2007 < http://www.flobeds.com/sleepWSJ.htm>.

[43] *Ordering Your Private World* 165.

[44] *Ordering Your Private World* 166-167.

[45] *Ordering Your Private World* 169.

[46] Consider *Color Me Beautiful* or *Color for Men* by Carole Jackson. On the market for two decades, these books still sound current.

[47] Psalm 139:13-16.

[48] When character Trofimov was asked by Libov Andreevna, "Are you still a student?" in Anton Chekhov's play, "The Cherry Orchard," this was his reply.

[49] Charles R. Swindoll, *Growing Strong in the Seasons of Life* (Portland, Ore.: Multnomah, 1983) 53.

[50] 2 Corinthians 4:16-18.

[51] Philippians 4:6.

[52] Philippians 4:7.

[53] Elisabeth Elliot, *Discipline, the Glad Surrender* (Old Tappan, N.J.: Revell, 1982).

[54] James 1:5.

[55] *Words to Love by* 31.

[56] Romans 8:37-39.

[57] 1 Thessalonians 5:17 (KJV).

[58] Kurt and I are unable to have children, but that hasn't stopped us from appreciating other people's children. In my speaking engagements, I often point out the fact that I was raised in a healthy home. My experience growing up becomes one of my qualifications to help others raise up their kids with purpose.

[59] "The State of the Family in Canada," Angus Reid Group (Ottawa: Angus Reid Group, 1994).

[60] C.S. Lewis, *The Four Loves* (New York: Harcourt, Brace, 1960) 71.

[61] Luci Swindoll, *You Bring the Confetti, God Brings the Joy* (Dallas: Word, 1986) 143.

[62] Nehemiah 8:12.

[63] Psalm 145:7.

[64] Isaiah 30:29.

[65] Luke 16:31-32.

[66] Joseph Bayly, "Psalm of Anticipation," *Psalms of My Life* (Colorado Springs: Chariot Victor, 2000).

[67] *You Bring the Confetti, God Brings the Joy* 39.

[68] Oswald Chambers, *My Utmost for His Highest: An Updated Edition in Today's Language* (Grand Rapids: Discovery House, 1992), July 28th entry.